Hume Cronyn
From the other side

AN ALTERNATIVE VIEW

by John M. Tettemer

Spiral Arrow Publications LLC
P.O. Box 9856
Newport Beach, CA 92658

ISBN-13: 978-0-9824532-0-9
ISBN-10: 0-9824532-0-5

Library of Congress Control Number: 2009927208

Cover photograph and all photographs on interior pages
are by the author and/or from his personal collection.

Printed and bound in the United States of America

First printing: August 2009

Table of Contents

Preface   **1**

I Introduction   **3**
Who Am I Really?
Myself as Seen from My Place in Spirit
Self Reflection and Discovery
Distortions, Ordinariness, Alter-Ego
A Guide for Many…Oneself as a Soul
Cultural Deception
Hume and John

II The Life I Led   23

The Call of Acting
Searching Insight, Long-Body,
    Teachings
Soul's Life and Ego
A Larger Perspective, Classroom,
    Schoolhouse
Role of Nature...Opening the Heart
Soul...The True Self Within
From Across the Veil

III Underneath It All   47

From the "Hereafter"
The Eternal Self...the Soul
The Classroom...An Inventory
The Real Unseen Me
The Goal Deep Within...Passion
Opening to Yourself

IV A Cry from Within   59

    Ego vs Soul
    Looking Within
    The Classroom
    A Time to "Be"
    Seeking Our Soul
    Re-empowering the Soul
    Our Connection to "All That Is"
    Rejection of the World of Spirit

V A View from Here   83

    Immortality
    Institutions
    Sin
    Freeing the Soul

VI The Blessings of This View for Others 141

Freedom
Going Within
"Nudges"
Nature
A Profound Teaching
Four Reasons

VII The Longer View 169

What Is to Be Learned?
We Are Eternal
Commitment to Our Soul's Goals
Passion
Service to the Evolution of Humankind
The Majesty of Life
A PRAYER

VIII Afterword 189

Author's Note

My name is John Tettemer. I am the "John" or "Johnnie" who is named in the narrative that follows.

This book is a work of the imagination in the sense that I am conveying to my readers the messages that were given to me by the spirit of Hume Cronyn.

It is an honor to have been asked by Hume Cronyn to bring his words through a channel and into print. In my case, amazingly, it was all done in the month of November 2008 while sitting in my car at a beach park in Southern California with an iPod that can be used as a recorder. I asked Hume to join me, and he and I became directly connected on a number of different days, as you will see. Hence, the substance of this book. It has been left as I heard it...almost verbatim.

There are others mentioned by Hume in his messages to me. His wife, whom he calls "Jessie," is Jessica Tandy, the actress, and the mother of "Susan" or "Susie" (my wife of over 49 years who is now in spirit). "Chris" and "Tandy" are the other Cronyn children who are also mentioned in the messages I received from Hume.

Further, he speaks of the "Bishop," who is John Moynihan Tettemer, now in spirit, an ex-Roman Catholic Bishop who was married to my mother Ruth. He also speaks of "Eileen," who is also in spirit. She is Eileen J. Garrett, a close family friend of the Tettemer clan, both here and there.

That is the "Cast"....

I knew these people in life, and now I pass along the messages I received from them in spirit.

Preface

10/15/2008, Honaunau, Hawaii

Hello Hume...I welcome our connection as it is to be...
Are you available to speak to me at this time?

Dear John...it seems that there is much to be said yet we are not yet connected...

Sit with me on the back lawn of the house you last knew, with pad, and we shall write. My last and first book were done in a place much different than today. I see life differently and wish sooo much to pass along a deeper, more important view of all that life is, for so many chase things with no lasting accord for they lack the perspective that puts life in a fuller and more wondrous perspective. Plays need be written about this for they communicate to many in heartfelt ways, and that is the purpose...is it not?

The title might be *Another View*, suggesting what is to follow which is another perspective...over from my current place that sees more clearly.

I

Introduction

10/15/2008, Honaunau, Hawaii, 2:44 p.m., 1:42

This is the 10/15 Honaunau discussion with Hume...
Clear voice...Excuse me...
I am reading from what I wrote before I put down the writing pad...

The title might be *Another View*, suggesting that I will follow with another perspective...one from my current place that sees more clearly what was and my commitment to it, and what might have been and my lack of commitment.

For I, like everyone else, as a creature...human creature...of a tangled life of great complexity, seeking to find oneself, opening those inner chambers and at the same time hiding, through performance (in my case the stage, screen, and all of those) the places one's stories...most personal stories…and the place of not mattering. For as we all speak, they are all that matters.

The greatest blessing of a piece of theatrical or film art is that a few may see themselves in it and in that realize a choice, exercise an option, heal an old wound, or other…

Because on the other side of the camera however much of the pain lingers, for acting under the direction of somebody else, for the purpose of a livelihood, no matter how artful, no matter how beautifully presented, does not allow the inner penetration of self to a place of meaning. The deeper penetration in my life came on and off through adventures that were not as I wished they would be. Rather than saying, ahhh, I welcome you for here is the depth of the information I need…to open myself…to change myself…to see myself in a perspective not of one seeking to heal others but to start a practice of healing oneself. And then, if called, going back to a place in the public arena where your material is "the" material —for that would be the ultimate truth of anybody's presentation to others and it need not be directed, for anyone who watches will know, feel and see and relent.

This is to bring this forward at this time to share an Alternative View or Another View of my life with Jessie, Susie, Chris and Tandy, some animals, many elaborate homes…often called "Hume's Follies" or "Cronyn's Follies," for yes they were. It was in those activities that I could lose myself in detail, in the illusion of control, in the illusion of creation and trust that, when accomplished, others would find them as I did, and behold, that never happened…

They were mine, my creations, my imagination, my yearnings, my endeavors, my obsessions…all designed in some way, as seen from today, to escape the simplicity of asking those extremely painful questions of: Who am I? What is this all about?

For I now see, without self condemnation, that the blessings of being who I was pushed me, relentlessly, toward achievement and that achievement was to be measured by public acceptance, the latter part being the trap.

Blessed Jessie…a magnificent actress…approached work, as has been written, from within. That had that effect on people.

I approached it from without and worked my way in...but only so far because to show my full vulnerability would be quite unacceptable.

Unacceptable to whom?

Me, of course!

For I was the one who carried the pain.

I was the one who hid the angst.

I was the one who was seeking to measure up...

I was the one seeking awards, in the hopes that others would tell me that I was not just alright, but excellent...

The families created from this form of obsession, with external approval, see it as a model and strive out into the world to emulate it. The difficulty of course is that passion may not be there. I am not speaking of Soul passion, I am talking about the passion of avoiding the pain of self discovery. So my addiction mutated into other forms of activity...by my children...for it seems they were dropped into the right family through their own series of awkward circumstances to experience what I and Jessie created, which in its own way was exactly counter to the very thing I was seeking.

Where was the closeness, love, and harmony of an internally oriented family that many miss? And I certainly did.

How then by seeking affirmation outside, almost at the level of an addiction, can children find the warmth of an internally oriented family?

It does not exist.

This initial draft is just that. Maybe bits and pieces that will be pulled together—a story here and a story there—and you, Dear John, I am not sure that we are fully connected. Worry not!

I suggest you type this, read it a time or two once you return to California. Find time that we gather again…and we will…for this is not a lengthy tome. This is a philosophical piece from a philosophical perspective and heartfelt, for I trust it will speak to many who seek to find themselves in other people's approval.

Does it mean, don't seek excellence in the outer world? NO!

Does it mean not contributing to the higher calling within, if it means support of externalities? A great NO!! NO!

It does mean analyzing closely, maybe daily, the intention, with honesty, courage, and bravery that far surpasses anything seen on the film or play or radio show...that skirts around the edges of the socially acceptable and unacceptable and painful, for they need intercourse amongst people to create what they have.

What I speak of is a lonely venture...most often alone.

Eventually we question ourselves about our intention and if we are blessed to be in touch with our passion (and we are clear how we have defined passion) for I can see it now as an under girding and edging like the primary wiring within each of us that seeks to carry the energy of life and express itself through us. And as we pass it moves on with us and as we return it returns also. For it is of the Soul. The warning here is that the mind, in its magnificence, or the ego, in its deceptive power, provide us with too much assistance in mis-defining our Soul's path. For many get themselves conned by themselves and do not realize that in life or in my case, after passing, the true essence of who I am only partly saw the light of day in that incarnation.

I wonder on, Dear John. Set this aside. You get a sense of what this is about…self reflection…and maybe because of the people knowing of the name, some will see themselves in the story and turn inward to greater self discovery, or modulate their relationship to the outer world, which later will allow less addiction to that and a greater opportunity of self discovery…for that is THE challenge in life. Little else matters.

We are wondrous and as we discover that is within ourselves, all else changes, including the magnificence of your Nature.

I've wondered on still further, Dear John…

Susie is here and sends her love and will be with you soon…

10/14/08, Honaunau, Hawaii, 8:36 p.m., 15:35

Another piece at Honaunau related to the discussion with Hume...

John, it is one thing for each of us to pursue our lives with intensity, and you know this well, seeking sometimes we know not what and yet when we find it, it can stroke us into believing that was the purpose. And yet from another vantage point, what was missed? It is for many the seeing and living life as a teaching and examining and reflecting on our lives, each step, each decision from the standpoint of... "What is the teaching?"

And in particular, the larger perspective.

For as you so eloquently described, the Soul passes on. I know that well...I'm in spirit with it.

Could this evolution be graded? Have we accepted the idea that it is a classroom and said, bring it on? Bring it on as a teaching...something to be added to what came into life before this life is over, for it contributes to the place of evolution of that Soul and in the next incarnation the Soul is better equipped and open for yet another teaching.

A haircut on Goat Cay.
Hume and John Tettemer.

For to consider our lives, in human form, as teachings, we are offered the opportunity to glimpse what our Soul is about, and as I am finding out there is nothing more profound than discovering oneself as a Soul. Greater meaning to life will come with us into the Hereafter, which is where I am, the greater the teaching. So when one considers how wonderful it would be if schools, parents, wisdom figures spoke as we are now of this being a teaching, for there is nowhere to go. If you recall...when we pass, the body is dropped and yet that is not the end. It is at that point that much of what we value in the common world is dissipated and yet what we valued and obtained in the Soulic world is retained and moved on.

So, my Alternative View that you may have wondered about coming to Honaunau at this late hour is to see that the Soul development is of great importance. I wish this brief book be carried forward to many, some of whom may see in it a gift of the observation that it is the Soul that has come into life using a body for its experiences. How wonderfully different that is than what most believe, should they have even an inkling about it at all.

What I direct to you now is sort of aloof and sophisticated for many and yet it is fundamental to all life. And, seen from this alternative place, what a wonder it would be if one contribution could be made to many...that they could see the Soul coming, be with them in passing as they dropped their body and that it is its future that they can affect in their presence on earth...

I will bring more to you Dear John... probably stories...but the wisdom may not exceed what we have discussed.

I feel you wondering if we are connected and as you have long written there is a thread amongst us all and much of what we speak of you are not imagining. And so with this pearl of wisdom or two from my alternative vantage point, I would like to thank you, and I know we will be speaking much more.

Return home to the place where you and Susie lived, and as time allows type up what has come through and let us ponder that and go on as we can, and as I wish, for there may be other pearls that we both feel warrant placing in this small book filled with photographs...a series of fundamental truths. New to the planet? Of course not, yet not built into the systems of life, of family, of community, of therapy, of showmanship at a level that is poignant enough to have any lasting effect. For how is it we would slay each other in the name of enhancing our Soul's passage through this lifetime?

I'm nudged to bring this now because there is a forum for telling these stories that would attend to my words in a different way than in New York. Then I would feel blessed for every and any one who was touched by the fundamentals set forth in the book, for now, dear one, know there is more. Know you may not understand all of this. I remember hearing of a mapless path. Let it go. Don't figure it out. Let it come forward as your other works…then yes, we are connected.

You are doing your Soul's business, Dear John, and it radiates from you like a great lantern.

Be blessed for now…

Hume-1 — 11/1/2008, Newport Beach, California

Good morning Hume, this is John.

I'm at the beach in Southern California as you know.

I feel my heart opening...wide open...to receive whatever it is that you would like to share related to construction, development of the book.

So I ask you to proceed...I invite you in...

Good morning Johnnie, this is Hume...

Wonder not...we are being connected.

There is much to bring forth. As I have mentioned I appreciate the time...and the love that you have provided.

It is now for us to work together and bring through much of this small book from a heartfelt place, a place of wanting the record straight and in straightening the record, helping many. For the difference between what we think we see and what is real, for many, is enormous, and living in that distortion creates great pain and a place of great wonder, a place of beauty, a place of love...and yet the distortion masks it all.

The distortion serves a smaller part of who we are, and that smaller part can dominate. For many, as we have moved away from the soil and the land and from your blessed Nature, they've removed themselves, some wittingly, some unwittingly, from the truth that is deep within and substituted what the small mind wishes to use to control, to animate, to sort, to judge. And that was my experience. For I too, as you know, was caught in the idea that I wasn't enough, yet that clearly was not true.

In seeking to become enough, I created a person out of who I am that was not who I am…a false image, you could say—of what life might be for me and others. Yes, deep within there was a crying, a deep crying, for an honest approach to what was around. And yet that honest approach might make me ordinary and some part of me could not stand to be ordinary, for fear of that being equal to "nothing."

So it was that much of my life was about constructing and maintaining whatever you might call an alter-ego or an alter-person, as I have mentioned briefly before. This person seeking to charm you, and to know me for who I wasn't, not who I was.

For who I wasn't became a public persona and my family persona many times. And that persona struggled, worked hard, performed nearly all the time and in so doing covered up the true inner aspect of self, that beautiful part of most that we could call "Soul."

Johnnie, it is the Soul that needs the fresh air of life. It is the Soul that needs to be found. It is the Soul that needs to be honored. And so your work, and ours in this case, is to assist others to understand that deeper within there is the truth of themselves...a "self," if you wish, or whatever you call it, and what you call it is not important.

Yet, it was difficult for me to find my way in and part of me was saying, "you are not enough." For what might I find if I went within?

I might find what the outer mind said I might...a weak, cringing little person, unable to deal with life in a meaningful way. Though there is that aspect of each of us, there is also deeper, below that, not a fearful little one but the smooth, loving blend of life that entered the body in the womb of the parent and came forward to be in this school to learn what life had to teach, to integrate what was useful to it, and which had perpetual value to it and then move on as it did at my death, and as I have.

For I see it now through very different eyes and it's for this purpose that you and I are working together. And let me say how I appreciate your willingness to move this forward, for it is the deception that has caused the problem for all of us, or most of us. It is the deception of the culture asking us to be something, absent the truth, within or without, for there is deception within also. It is an echo of the deception without.

Or if the community and its culture were one that was open to an honest relationship to what is within, much of what we struggle with would disappear. However, that is not our lot.

In the teaching of the Soul through our life experiences, we have the opportunity of digging deep within. As I mentioned, I was fearful. It was unacceptable, maybe deadly. I would certainly impact those around me, who I pretended were relying on me for everything, every breath. What a falsehood that was, for it is the very choking off of myself that choked off those around me. That choking restricts the flow of air, does it not? The restriction of the flow of air restricts the body's ability to inhale and exhale its fullest…and those are the breaths of God, as I now know.

It is this book, Dear John, that needs the title for now of *An Alternative View*…that is fine…

And so we have started…

Hume and John

11/3/2008

It is another cloud studded sky—and the temperature lower and the air clear—beautiful as the work with Hume deepens and his wonderful thoughts about reality stream forth. It is an honor to receive his thoughts and eternal wisdom, for that it is, and soon it will fill a small folder and be ready for publication...maybe by month end.

It is a great honor as said to be asked to carry forward Hume's contribution to modern society, for his name is well known as is his work and that will cast the seeds widely for many, and yes maybe in more than our language.

It is early in the New Year when the photos and the text merge into the small tome he seeks and will have for I joyfully said yes. That is nearly sacred for me and him. We converse and he said bring questions and so I will, for it is being true to his vision that I seek...poetic, maybe, yet it is an honor.

The families will have their personal reactions and so be that. It must be, and also it is his wisdom that they will honor over time, for he cuts through the fluff.

Hume speaks…

"You will, Dear John, take it into the world. The others are too connected. Why burden them?"

Above much, Hume has offered me the chance to prove to myself that I can channel him here in California. The material is very clear and direct; it completes any questions about what was going on.

Hume speaks…

"Yes, John you channel and well and are mature and wise enough to understand it and leave it alone."

Thank you, Hume

Hume, I ask about the next session…
How about Wednesday November 5 at the same beach?

Hume speaks…

"O.K. See you there."

II

The Life I Led

Hume-1 — 11/01/08, Newport Beach, California

It is from the wonder of my childhood that I moved directly and indirectly into the idea of performance.

When I look at it philosophically today, it was not a linear approach to acting, but underneath it all there was a knowledge that acting was important and what a metaphor that has been and is for the life led. For acting suggests, in its very nature, the notion that what the performers are doing is different than who they are at their core.

To act is to present something which may or may not be authentic to "Self"…and that is the nature of the assignments, and there were many. On screen in the early days, the theater, which I loved the most, and then writing and the theater, and then writing for great people to act. These marvelous stories that were created are often stories of "Self," but put in other people's hands to act out, to be different than who they were when they were presented the material that we scribed from what we thought was imagination. Often, as you know, it was brought through from thoughts deep within...

As it has turned out, the successes were abundant. The intensity of the commitment to the work, my involvement with Jessie, brought us both to the front of the industry. For we both, in our own ways, were committed, dedicated students of the art of acting in all sorts of ways and in many incarnations. We associated with those in New York, Hollywood, London and elsewhere who were also committed to the arts and through this activity we became part of the "state-of-the-art" of acting, which means that whatever brought us to it was being fulfilled. This desire was being fulfilled and the awards and financial well-being and freedom to presumably be who we were followed abundantly—and for that one can say thank you, thank you, thank you!!!

Hume says: "It is well worthwhile, Johnnie, to add names of plays and pictures and books...writings to a section here...in some way."

At Hume's request, the following is a small sampling of various projects that led to nominations and/or awards for an Academy Award, Tony Award, Emmy Award, and Academy of Science Fiction, Fantasy, and Horror Award, and his other acting, writing, directing, and producing credits:

Rope

Portrait of a Madonna

The Play's the Thing

Under Capricorn

The Dollmaker (with Susan Cooper)

Four Poster

Foxfire

Age-Old Friends

Broadway Bound

To Dance with the White Dog

There Was a Crooked Man

The Gin Game

Honky Tonk Freeway

The World According to Garp

Cocoon

The Pelican Brief

Camile

People, A Musical Celebration.

12 Angry Men

Angel Passing

The world responded to the intensity of our interest in performance and we were offered and often performed magnificent plays, toured with them, and some film work came our way. Film work was not our favorite but it paid the bills, and our connection with many of the historic great names of Hollywood was rewarding for those that were acting…and we were.

John adds…*Hume indicated, as an aside, that much else can be found in his Memoir,* A Terrible Liar.

Hume-2 — 11/05/08, Newport Beach, California, 9 a.m.

*Good morning Dear Hume. This is our time again—
November 5, '08...*

*As asked, I have typed up what came before and I find
it beautiful, succinct, direct, strong, and appropriate. And I
welcome, as we move forward, whatever is added to this.
Know that I feel quite well prepared to bring forward the
small tome.*

Good morning John, this is Hume. Thank you for the
wonderful work for I feel as you do, emotionally connected. It is a wonder, for it is through unseen energy, a
subject so dear to you and so real to all and so misunder-
stood by many. For we are connected from many decades
ago, and here is an example: that we live together, you and
I. No, not physically in the same room but energetically in
the same room, so to speak. For in these fields of energy,
distance means nothing. It is as though we are next door to
each other, or that I sit next to you in your car.

So, know by the feel of the emotion that we are connected and we will over a series of gatherings, such as this

and the last one, bring forward just what is needed—little editing required, some guidance from me and off you go, Dear John, for you know the way.

This material is very close to your perception of "what is" and so it is easy to work with. Only occasionally do I stray off, and yet I find you find that useful also.

A number of questions and answers were exchanged between Hume and John about the production of this book.

JOHN—*I am ready to proceed, Hume, as you are.*

HUME—It is again with my great thanks, Dear John, that you record and transcribe and are ready to take to the world these thoughts from where I am.

As you have seen so far, they differ greatly from the way I lived and it is that dichotomy, maybe a misunderstanding of life or even deeper, maybe a desire to avoid the profundity of it, for it shined too bright a light into my life at that time and might have brought down the house of cards that I had built. For without doubt the wonder of what my life was about, that may be appealing to many, and maybe used as a beacon for some, was far from what was deep within. And that is what it is today—deep within—and that is what counts. This time on earth that you are experiencing, Dear John, is just that: it is time on earth. There is a continuation of what you call the long body that knows that this is just a visit and that the end is not the end. It is the beginning of the next phase. It is this long-body continuity that puts things in perspective, that allows people, or energies such as mine, as we pass to reflect on "what was that"? and in a few remarkable cases bring it through, maybe in times of need, maybe at times of family panic, maybe other times.

I bring it through as a teaching about a teaching—funny words of course. My life on earth was a teaching for me. I learned I could find my way through life, acceptable to many, idolized by a few, by being quite public in what they thought I did, which was to act, and inherently as we have discussed, acting is not being oneself. And there is the crux of the basic issue, for it is "oneself" that is brought to the earth to experience life, to be affected by it, to learn from it.

In each incarnation there is a sort of agenda that is chosen and life revolves most around that agenda. The effect of the agenda and the usefulness of it to the Soul varies depending on the individual's ability to access the entire program, so to speak, of their school while there. Few do, as you know, Dear John. Most are unaware of the school, most are unaware of the "long-body," most believe the end is the end and that the rest are just stories made up through good writing or television today.

Part of what I write about is to connect my name to this miraculous aspect of the long-body—connect my name to the miraculous aspect of this being a teaching—a place where there is something to be learned by the soul that lives the long body and that wishes to provide the opportunity for growth and to be overwhelmed if need be by the ego, as we talked. Yet, the overall intention is not to have the ego direct traffic, as you might say, but rather to let the desire of the Soul come forward and guide the family or individual in their pattern of daily living to have experiences that nourish the Soul in its progression and evolution to a higher and higher state of being.

So this is what it is about. It is about each of us coming to the earth plane for experience to learn—to learn about themselves and the sense of their Soul and also to learn about themselves in a sense of those things that inhibit the Soul's progress, such as aspects of inferiority, aspects of ego, various devices within the mind and the body that prohibit the movement forward that we all might seek. For many would rather be controlled by ego for fear that they might discover within themselves a truth that was damaging or frightening...more frightening than being minimized in their life path to a place of plodding, plodding, plodding and then passing. For the excitement of life John, as you know it, and as you know, can be great. Merely making contact with a plant or a flower or a bug can lift an entire day forward, for it is inexplicable. Its dimension, its wisdom, its source of incredible learning, carried down generation after generation after generation in its simple form, we might say, and yet the complexity of what it knows intuitively is beyond our imagination. So we project onto it our own lives and wonder about how it does what it does and yet it does. It has evolved, and that is the secret. The secret is the evolution of the Soul. The Soul seeks to evolve and provides opportunity for us as we carry it forward, embodied, in your world. In my world, I live in the Soul and see through its eyes a very different perspective of what life on earth can be, for it is as magical as we choose to make it. There is nothing in the universe that comes close to the magnificence of earth at every level—and that is every level—and yet the mind of man can vilify, can stomp on, can disregard the amazement of it all. And I mean that disregarding, blows away, to use a term, the incredible gift of coming to earth for that experience. And many wait in line for it, knowing that on their arrival they will see, feel, smell, touch and live in this incredible environment that is unique. Seek this environment elsewhere in our solar system, Dear John, and you will find it does not exist. That alone should bring a sense of awe to many, to many, to many, and yet it is easy to get caught up in family details—the nature of the front door, the new car, changing a bathroom fixture, growing children. The smallness of life gets to be the dominant aspect of life, because people are listening to the culture they are within and that culture is based on economics and limited wisdom. As you see the greater the college time for many we see little growth in wisdom, maybe some book learning that is probably immediately lost but little that can carry forward into a meaningful contribution to their life, other than the passage to some other grail.

For there is more wisdom in watching nature, Dear John, as you well know, than there is in any classroom. For the classrooms are way behind, they don't speak to the individual Soul. They speak to an average, in material put in awkward words, with awkward ideas that are also fabricated to the place where no one knows what the truth is, but they teach it because something has to be taught, and that is a myth. Far better one camps on a hilltop for several years, or lives on an island for several years to find out what life is about. For the urban systems deliberately insulate one from life so that they can be manipulated and, though this sounds negative, what I speak to is the antithesis of that. What I speak to is the antithesis of my acting. Few could sense who Hume is through his acting, and it is about who Hume is that I wish to speak. Not because I am Hume, but because I am using myself as a model of the difference between what appears in life, in the routine, mundane world and the truth behind it all, as I now see it from this wonderful place in spirit.

I speak then much about larger perspective, the perspective held by few and yet dearly important for there are no institutions that I am aware of that speak what I speak, for their very future would be threatened by the candor and the personal nature of these journeys that we take into our classroom, for they again average and average and average to the place where there is nothing left for the individual other than average, and this is so far above average. This is magnificent! The perception of life on earth from here is of an attractive, wonderful, beautiful, graceful opportunity to experience aspects of life needed for the evolution of the Soul. It is to that that I wish to direct any reader of this material through the admission, if you wish, and the wonderful free admission, that the human they may have known on earth, even though the name may be world wide, was not the Hume that Hume was.

It was a Hume that had learned an art, a craft, and a way to escape, and it worked. One of the stories, of course, is that having done that, somewhere along the line in life one trips into oneself and that opens and explores and redeems all of that. In my case that was not the case. Certainly there were times of great insight, and nothing like the insight that is available from where I am today, for there was quite clear direction coming from me to you, Dear John, to write the truth as I bring it through. For my life as seen from today is very different from the life I lived caught as I was in the world's machinery, the world's interpretation of who I was, and that was fragile and needed to be protected at all costs for fear that somebody would understand who I am.

Let me say clearly now: there is not one of us here, or in reading this, that is not far greater than they can imagine, FAR greater than they can imagine. For it is a small aspect of our self that judges, criticizes and all and it gets so used to that that it forgets who is doing that. Once one moves away from the need to criticize and opens to merely being one of many, one of many animals, if you wish, inhabiting this magnificent planet...that one can see that being here at all is a blessing and that opening to that blessing and the nature and realization of what being here means, there is transformation and that transformation essentially is the education of the Soul through this classroom—the classroom of wonder, the classroom of the smallness of human life, the classroom of color, of sound, of magnificence, of height, of low, of pressure, of no pressure, of speed and no speed, of physical touch—many of these things are absent in the time between incarnations and so we long for them. We long for the life that many on earth reject. They reject it through fear, fear of who they are. If they realized who they are as an energetic body, they would realize that the gift they are receiving is truly a gift from the gods.

And the gods are behind all of this, for however you define God there is an energetic of great height, breadth, depth, width, and infinite complexity beyond the human mind to understand that sees the flow of energies, that works with the flow of energies in its own hierarchy, for its own objectives, for the purpose of supporting mankind and the evolution of the Souls of all. For this slice of the universe is about Soulic evolution. And, it is to that that we address ourselves, as we think, in this rather mystical world I speak of now. Why all of this? The answer is, "the bigger calling is the evolution of our Soul."

How, Dear John, you may ask, on other's behalf when they read this, how do we know all of this?

From this place of spirit it is clear to see the stress, the dysfunction, the desire unmet, the awkwardness of loving, the effect on the planet of human life—that much is now out of balance—and it is the balance that keeps the classroom in place. If we damage the classroom, we damage the opportunity for Soulic evolution on this wonderful, beautiful planet you call earth and the energies afoot are not apt to have that happen, and though they greatly respect free-will, there is a limit to that also.

So, I know not what the boundaries of this are. I am not that wise or that seasoned here, but suffice it to say that there are energies afoot that oversee this and in overseeing it do judge its long-term stability, for as a schoolroom they require its existence. And the quality of and the experiences available through the schoolroom are important, for if they fail, Soulic evolution slows down at the human level and difficulties pursue, including potential damage to the planet.

And recall we are only one animal, if you wish, that inhabits this planet, that has inhabited for some time, and yet the planet has experienced many other deep evolutions of time, and space, and inhabitants.

We may say, "well that is nice...but not important to us," and I would say in response, "maybe," but it is my experience, Hume's experience, that the magnificence of "what is" requires our devotion. For though we may not be here for an eternity in this physical body, we have an obligation to our children, and their children and the evolution of the planet to leave it without footprints. As we came, so we leave it, and if that is done consciously there will be great joy, for it is in balancing what we do in all cases that allows the schoolhouse to continue and grow and learn and evolve the materials and designs and all the things that man encounters and wishes, because it morphs along with that, and that is appropriate. The school house adjusts to time and events and it is now, particularly through your eyes Dear John as one interested in nature, that man is challenging nature to its limits and from where we sit that is another folly. For man is unconscious to his impact on nature in a way that he will act on for fear of losing power over nature and of course, by his very acts, that is what is happening. He is reworking nature through his lack of care and his abuse to a place where it can no longer respond to his highest calling, and in fact will respond negatively in the not too distant future unless dramatic changes are made in his approach to life, which means controlling his impact, adjusting his footprint, honoring life at all levels, including your wonderful snail and bugs, your little friends, and your larger friends, for they too inhabit this planet. They too are required to keep the planet in balance. It is that that we need to know about. Some reject the idea of a cat, for example, eating a bird in the back yard, as you often do, Dear John, and yet part of that is a balancing device that is in nature. It can over-swing one way or another but there need be balances and nature seeks those in its own cyclical way, for all is cyclical, like our incarnations, or coming from and to school. It is in honoring those cycles, and honoring all participants brought into this by nature, that we support the highest journey for all.

It is my desire that people read this book and they are open to this discussion of today through my very honest and loving admission that who they thought I was, I was not. And yet I could perform and did, so they were served and I was too at some level. The reason, of course, for bringing this forward is to allow many to reflect on who they are at depth, for that is where the Soul resides and it is where the Soul resides that needs attention. The outer world is the outer world and our response to the outer world need reflect more of the Soul's intention, and to have that happen requires that we get in contact with our Soul.

The beauty of who we are, all of us, regardless, yes, some need more time in school than others, etc, etc, there is unlimited diversity amongst us all and it is the Soul's evolution in this incredibly complex, diverse universe of human nature, and human beings that needs our attention now.

So by presenting myself as something deep "within" that is different than what they saw "without," I ask others to think of their own circumstance, a circumstance of who they believe they are as seen by others and get candid and honest about it. For in that candor and honesty they will find that part of them knows they are acting also, no matter who they are—the barber, the welder, the farmer, the brain surgeon—they are acting, for deep within they will find their Soul. Some, fortunately, will find that they are in sync with their Soul's desire. They are living the life that the Soul wishes led, meaning that the dominancy of the ego has been set aside in someway in favor of the Soul's journey and that that has worked for them to provide a livelihood for themselves, family, whoever, in keeping with the progression of the long body...and that is wonderful.

We have, however, drifted a long way from a time of worshipping nature, for it is in that worshipping of nature that we find ourselves. It moves us closer to our fundamental truths than any classroom, historical novels, or whatever.

So, one might wonder why it is that being in nature as you champion so much, Dear John, is important.

The answer very fundamentally, as I see it, is that it brings us back close to earth, earth energies, water energies, fundamental life, and it is near fundamental life that the Soul operates. Not that it isn't highly complex, and it is, but its energies are closer to those of nature than it is the ego-based mind of man. So it is seeking out who we are, as we strip away who we are not, but think we are, leaving us standing, if you wish, bare or nude before nature of which we are a Soulic part.

This for me, Dear John, is a very poignant piece, for it creates a picture in my mind of humans out acting, trying to be something acceptable to others so that their little mind feels at ease and of course it never does. For deep within this other aspect, close to nature, close to what they walk on, what they breathe, what they drink, what they eat is the fundamental aspect of life, of them, their Soul.

Many can report an event or two in their life where they felt open to something much larger than them-selves...and it was at those times that the mind was set aside, the heart opened and the heart knows. Its very nature is connected to nature. By that I mean the complexity, and the totality of the energies of life, not the creation of man's mind in structure, competition, warfare, hatred, based on the small aspects of the ego mind, but based on the long-body evolution of humankind. The heart connects all, and all is related to the Soul, that deep inner aspect of self that is unique in its totality and can be hidden by modern life, as we mentioned through all the processes of the mind and the physical aspects of the world. And yet recall that many can hibernate in natural settings and find wonderment in their lives for they get near, or some may contact the Soul in its life, the Soul in its development, the wonder of that energetic relationship to all that is over all time, for it is all one in its natural form.

I have moved, Dear John, off into the greater realm. It is this greater realm that I know you vibrate in. As to that I celebrate, for the notion that we are more deep within and that that more is connected to more are fundamental truths, fundamental truths that once again need to be brought forward through the smoke and haze of the modern world, of complex organization and law and theory and goodies that have made life unmanageable for most.

The pain and suffering and warfare of the world suggest that either man was brought here to destroy himself, use his intelligence to create better ways to kill himself, or he is off track—for where I am, he is off track and represents one of the most magnificent creatures imaginable when working from the place of heart or Soul.

And if this book has meaning, and I believe it does, it suggests that this one human has seen through the veil and now lives on the other side of the veil and looks back through it and sees that each individual seems, with choice, to create an artificial world for apparent safety, for parent acceptance, to receive love, to reproduce, etc. and yet deep within, that is all acting. It is not real, for what is real is deep within, it is the life of the Soul, the connection and worshipping, if you wish, of exactly what nature has brought forward. It need not be tampered with by man. Man at your level is a relatively short-term visitor to all of this, as you found out from Iona. Those teachings from Iona are being brought forward through you, Dear John, for they speak to a simpler time, and I support that, a time where we do not judge in terms of things. We judge in terms of harmony. Yes, we will live and yes we will compete here and there. The nurturing of nature, the co-existence with nature is fundamental to all life, for that way only can it exist.

And so we are properly chosen to work together, my friend from that island in the Bahamas. From that time forward this was blessed to be, only waiting for the events to uncoil, and here we are now, with maybe another chapter or two and there will be many more, several more. And it is to you I salute, my love, my energies (tears) and know you are guided, know you are loved, and yes even protected.

Susie is here, sees your vulnerability and sends her deepest love, for she too knows of your wisdom and caring of nature, your love for her and your family. Be blessed by us both, for we honor your path, which is not easy…impossible for many…but you were born to it, Dear John. Know that and know that it is guided and protected.

For now…

And we will answer your questions as the time requires.

Blessings.

III

Underneath It All

Hume-1 — 11/01/08, Newport Beach, California

Upon one's death and passing, as it is said, part passes and part does not. The body remains, as we know, but I am now in the, so called, HEREAFTER. That part passed, and as I look back, if you wish, from where I am to what was and how it unfolded, I find there was an enormous gulf between who I created, through the idea of acting, and the blurred line between the script and my real life. For my real life became acting also and probably always was to the place where I was unaware, quite unaware. Except every once in a while, the deep pang that I feel, quite unaware that there was another person within me, so to speak, what you Dear Johnnie would call an energetic, that sought expression but was tamped down by the need of the time, the need of wealth, the need of recognition, the need to be right, the need of being in the world, the need of being O.K. with the family...

47

And now it is in full bloom, that part—we can call it Soul and it sees from this perspective the magnificent job that was done in creating this alter-ego aspect. Refined to the max, so to speak, for like most people who pretend to be something that maybe they are deeply not, it was my charge to do that for myself and also for the characters I played, and in becoming proficient at it it bled into being proficient with the other. The result of course being almost a blur between the acting person, the person I am, or lived life to be, all the while disregarding what I now know is deep within, which is the person represented by the Soul, the rich, eternal aspect of Self, the smooth, somewhat frictionless aspect of Self, that part that works with an intuitive flow of life and allows life to move it as life flows around it, through it, above it, below it and seeks its acceptance of what is without changing the character of the Soul, for the Soul has its own unique character over the millennia.

The nature of these times in the earth plane, for me the actor, is a chance for the Soul to learn, for it is the classroom. What I wish to leave with the reader is that this was a harsh classroom for me for what it appeared that I was is very different than what I am, and yet I knew that not. Even those poetic words are interesting only in glimpses. That strange time we have on occasion, here and there, when one could reveal oneself to oneself, that I sensed that there was something more, but the world around didn't see that for I wasn't sure I could manage it, control it, direct it, and act it properly. So it is left in the back room, so to speak, and there it moldered until my passing and now I am it and wish forcefully to express its interest that the beauty of acting, in terms of telling a story, is wonderful. These stories need to be told and they need to be told through acting, for they are often other people's stories. The other part, however, is that one needn't become an actor. At a deep level, one needs to become the expression of the Soul, and for many in today's world those words are not available to them to consider, let alone seek.

So, as an extreme polarity it is of great interest as I sit in the Hereafter, to recommend strongly that there are chances for each of us at some time, through some process, to reach inside, to listen to what is there and recognize the beautiful peace, and love, and appreciation of life that we embody and the eternal nature of it. For that is where I am, and so I represent an extreme and by that extreme may be a good lesson for others. The acting looked sublime to some, certainly professional to many, of many decades duration, and yet…what was it within?

Did it serve the person that was carrying the message? Was the messenger served, so to speak? And the answer for me was NO! For it was all about reflecting to the community what it wanted to see, not who I was, for had I been who I was, I would have been fearful in approaching that—reject it and walk away as I did on more than one occasion—for to own the depth of who I was without knowing who I was is fearful and it is that fear that drives so many of us away or prevents us from approaching the beauty of who we are deep within.

So much is written about this, and as I mentioned earlier…I was prepared to become vulnerable, in terms of the characters I presented. That vulnerability got into my own life at some level, but only at some level, for to become fully vulnerable would disarm me from having the tools to deal with life as I have constructed it, not as it had demanded, but as I constructed it, for we are not victims of our lives. There are choices we make based on fear, based on family culture, that can restrict us from approaching life from the depth of who we are and the wonder of that, and the restriction reduces the opportunity for life to be a teaching, for we don't allow the experience of life access to our Soul. We seek to separate them: keep the Soul submerged. Because we don't understand it, we are fearful of it or believe it would not represent us the way we might wish and much of that, Dear John, and others that read, is incorrect. The Soul can be seen, itself, by other Souls and even in the absence of any great wisdom, many feel a person, as they live their Soulic life, as something special and amazing and to be emulated, so the ultimate acting could be being oneself, and what a wonder that would be.

Could you imagine if people became what their Soul was here to experience?

The teachings would change, if they were needed at all, for the experiences would not be one of creating a "presence" to be present with. It would just "be," relaxing into who is present and peace and love, giving and receiving without pretense, without the need for judgment, without the need for fear, because there is nothing to fear in the eternal life that is within us…it goes on. Mistakes are not judged by the Soul. The fullness of life adds to the Soul's passage and that Dear John, as you are writing with your father, is of great importance.

How might one approach all this you ask?

From this small tome please first consider the applicability of these ideas or my experiences to your life, for many will find, without the refinement, that the art of Hollywood or the art of New York, that much of their life is crafted around becoming acceptable to someone or something, or some culture or some belief system or some religion, some of which or none of which may be at the core of one's being.

An initial step then is identifying, each day, to the extent that one can, those aspects of self that are designed, practiced, rehearsed, examined, reexamined, and turned around, looked at over and over again by the mind, the ego aspect as it seeks to create an outcome. To control? Yes. To be all right? Yes. Because it has defined what "all right" is and somehow how to be secure in one's future.

And all of this is, of course, an illusion, beginning with the last one. The future is undetermined and can not be controlled. That is a rule beyond all rules, and yet how much of our energy goes into trying to secure, through manipulation of ourselves into our community, into our relationships, into our finances, what we think the future will be.

So we predict a future out of our mind, out of our fear, and seek to manifest it and in that very manifestation can squelch many of the opportunities for new experience, change, adventure, full living of life to be with us and for a full expression at that time of our Soul's intention and the love of life that it brings forward without judgment, without ego, and in peace.

And so in constructing this daily inventory, if you wish, of how it is we seek to preserve ourselves or create a world around us that is artificial. And many will say yes, but it is endemic or pandemic. How could I possibly find another me? And that is where quiet time, Dear John, as you now know, some people call it meditation, whatever it is...listening to dreams. There are many, many ways of starting to honor what might be within you, which I know is an alternative reality connected to your Soul, the wholeness of who you really are eternally. You might say that is nice but what does that have to do with today? And the answer is as you approach it, everything, for as you change your perception of what goes on around you, you open yourself to yourself and that is a profound thought, for we become our perceptions. Interesting isn't it? And yet the Soul is always there and as we seek to become our perception of our Soul's path, which would be our passion in life, our life shifts because we see it differently, and seeing it differently it affects us differently, and in affecting us differently we can open to it differently. As we open to it differently, it becomes us, fully, not stuck away in the closet hoping nobody sees it because we fear what it might be and in fact it turns out to be most of who we are, a wonderment without doubt for each and everyone!

So we watch ourselves. What are we doing to create an artificial "me" to be with an artificial "you" in an artificial "world"?

We also seek out our passion for it is in passion, that you speak of so much John, that the energies of the Soul are expressed, not what we would think others would like to have us do—and that is a very scary line to draw—but rather the line of, "I think that if I had only one thing to do in the world it would be X." Maybe it is gardening, maybe it is photography, maybe it is caring for Nature, whatever it might be, but like a wonderful vacation pursuit that, even for moments, starts to open the door, and when the energies start to flow, they may trickle through at first...drop, drop, drop, or trickle, trickle, trickle. But as the door opens, they will displace—the energies of the Soul's passion will displace the need to be something for others because you realize being something for yourself in response to the Soul is itself a magical, fulfilling experience, infectious, addictious (my word), addiction oriented, obsessing. It takes over and is real. It is loving. It is an experience that many never have and yet it is available through work to find ourselves, not through acting, not through pretending, no matter how elegant that is, but through doing the work from deep within.

You may ask in my case would that mean I couldn't have acted? No! To the contrary!! Can you imagine those few who can act from the place of the Soul's passion? Not to hide from life through acting but their passion is in fact to bring the energies of the Soul forward onto a stage or onto film or in music singing with a heart wide open.

You know it when you see it, Dear ones, that is always the case but how few get there. I did not.

So I seek now through this small volume to remind you of the wonder of what my life appeared to be and show you essentially what the shadow to that is, the shadow being the reverse that is held in an opposite energy, that has always driven to protect what I thought was my self or my vulnerability, through excellence in a field of acting, of pretending to be something essentially that I was not, and that is wrong.

The question behind this all is the motive. If it comes from the Soul, it is beautiful, God given so to speak. If it comes from defense, it is a living hell within and that can be avoided and so I speak to that...I speak to that...I speak to that...

Enough for now, Dear Johnnie, please type up what you have; ask questions about it.

You wonder slightly if I am present. Know that the images that come to you are coming from somewhere and I can assure you of my presence. Yet I honor that constant little voice that asks, is that me or am I making this up? Or is this Hume?

See how it sounds as you type it up and let us join again, and again, and again.

And again my heart goes out to you with thanks. As you can tell, this book will come together relatively quickly.

Recall also as you have been touched that you are open to receive and it is for me to bring this story forward, for you to process…and so we have started.

My love to you…

The Radio Room, Children's Bay Cay.

IV

A Cry from Within

Hume-3 — 11/09/08, Newport Beach, California, 46:28

Good morning Hume. This is John at our beach rendezvous place...Sunday...

As we connect I have some questions.

Let me start by saying that I truly honor your willingness to bring this material forward and feel it is a privilege that you are willing to do it with me, so I want you to know that.

Good morning John, this is Hume as we share wonderings, honoring the pleasure of this deep-felt connection you now feel in your heart, because your heart just opened, Dear John. And know that it always will at these gatherings, if not before you get here. However, being human, there we are.

You have several good questions...let us go through those.

JOHN—*Is it useful for me, Hume, to start putting this material into the context of the folder?*

HUME—As you see fit. No hurry, but if it organizes for you then I think that would be useful. You will find it fits together quite neatly. We can see it, for we hold it and as strange as that may seem, trust that that is the truth…and you get a mild chill when I say that.

JOHN—*Another question from me Hume, is, am I catching faithfully what you are bringing through?*

HUME—More than faithfully, Dear John, it is almost verbatim. In fact what else could it be, for what you are speaking is what I send you and the channel is clear. So yes, and as you read it you see that it is almost letter perfect, not from our collective wisdom, but from the clarity of the channel. So trust that all is in order, for it is, and there is more to come, of course.

JOHN—*My final question is, is the rhythm of our gatherings here, every once or twice a week, working for you?*

HUME—Ahhhh, I have much time. It is you that is doing the work. Make the rhythm fit your life, Dear John. Worry not about my timing. A more direct answer is yes, this is fine but have it be fine with you, for it is tiring also. Ahh yes...

Let me move on now since you have exhausted your list...

There has been much said about life and death, much said about the burden of being in life without the full recognition that your father, the Bishop, and you are working on, that there is far more to the larger pattern than the smallness of what we think is our allotted time on earth and this is important. It is an important piece to bring into this book for it changes the perspective of what is driving us. We have talked as you know about performance, appearing to be something we maybe aren't, seeking of course sufficient wealth to be comfortable if possible and for some that works. For many it does not. Nothing wrong with the pursuit.

There then becomes the time of stepping back, which you and I are enjoying at this time, and saying "is this the bigger picture to be looked at or have we gotten caught in yet another level of smallness?" So let us introduce into this text the notion of a largerness. I like that word "largerness"...never heard it...for a largerness would be wondering if, as we move into our life there is more to it than growing up, having children, working, and passing. For it is as we have learned from the Bishop, a school, a school for learning, a school for the evolution of our Soul. That, Dear John, is exactly what I have found, for I went into that incarnation with some wonderment from my family's life and some burdens of size, what I thought was intellect, and yet found through competition and pursuit in excellence and quality I couldn't address life the way it was presented to me without any understanding, as we have previously discussed, about what was going on "within." For it is what's going on within that creates the authentic part that is without, and it is what's going on within that addresses the life and evolution and development of the Soul. The Soul's life transcends any one physical life. So, to the extent that we focus deeply on how to defend ourselves in this ruthless or heartless or financial or reward driven life, we have ignored, abandoned the very part of who we are that is most important....the Soul.

For the soul cannot speak in a way to overcome that enormous thing called an ego. Though small in size, it is large in energy. The result being that the soul cannot compete with the ego. The result is that those of us who find ourselves at some disadvantage, whether we have defined it or others have defined it for us, or the culture has defined it for us strive out to overcome that and in many cases do not conscript that beautiful part of us that could float through that aspect of life with little effort. For the conscription of the soul to live life, to be in balance with life, to see life as a teaching, and a piece of the long, long body, as you like to say, of multiple generations of incarnation, that is what it is about. And so it is in that long-body that we find that who we are in any one lifetime is not all that significant, and yet we act in each step of these lives on earth, so to speak, as though our life depended on it. I am playing with words here. In a sense our life does depend on it, but the long-body life does not and that long body beautifully worked out, beautifully said, beautifully lived will allow us to see our life on earth as literally a classroom which the Bishop likes to speak of. For it is here that there are things to learn but from a perspective of being a student, not being the master of the class or in control or designing the future. For none of that happens as you well know. Tomorrow is not evident today. Though we wish things on to it, we have no assurance of those happening.

So it is stepping back into the life of the Soul, from this forced life of the ego, where there is peace, and love and the development of ourselves for future incarnations and the time in spirit, which is where I now am. I belatedly found this out, Dear John, after passing, though much of it…though I spoke of it, and even wrote about it a little bit, was not inherent in my way of dealing with life. There was too much pain, too much suffering, too much overreaction to all of that, and maybe too little attention to the Soul's intention, of that I am now sure.

So where from here on all of this?

We ask the reader to set aside time each day, each week, each month, but frequently enough to impact their way of connecting to life and stepping back, maybe in nature, or some friendly place where one feels necessarily and inherently comforted, to buffer the outer world from us—that frankly artificial world that prevents us from seeking and finding the inner world we speak of—and spending time there seeking within the inner world to ask ourselves frequently, "what is the teaching I am here to obtain?"... "how can I support that?"... "how can I encourage more of it?"... "are my relationships with my work and my life and my children and animals and nature consistent with the schoolhouse, or have I created follies here and there and everywhere in an attempt to distract myself from my inner truths as a way of trying to be O.K. from a mental standpoint with myself?"...

Time alone...what is to be done there? Therein lies the tale. There is very often nothing to be "done," for done implies the idea of work or accomplishment or energizing some particular part of self toward an objective that is defined. This, unlike that, is a time of "nothing to do." It is a time of "being" for you will find—many will find—as you have, Dear John, that these times will start to speak, maybe a little bit here, maybe a little bit there, and those need to be attended to and put on a piece of paper. For however small they may be, they are a crack in the door or crack in the door opening leading to a wider and wider flow of energy coming through to speak to you of who you are, and it is this revelation that begins to open the heart wider and wider and wider.

It cannot happen in a group. It cannot happen in an organization. It cannot happen through ego power. It cannot happen by being the president or something else. It happens alone, by yourself, thinking of yourself, feeling into your self at a level where the mind and therefore the ego has little to say.

It is this piece of therapy, if you wish, that is so simple that it requires nothing but commitment. It doesn't need professional help, doesn't need doctors and medical things and pills and injections and special practices. It needs what nature provided abundantly, and that is nature. It needs each to seek out times to be alone and in a setting that is natural where the energies can flow from the earth to the body, body to the earth, plants to body and body to the plants, birds and on and on, where the wind can blow through your hair without worry about being mussed up or anything, a sense of being natural—for natural and nature are closely connected—no pretense, just being present and quiet. And that alone for many is an extreme challenge, for their life has been one of chaos, noise, activity, furtive this and that, with the result that they are never at peace. And the system that we live in, Dear John, as you well know is one of continuously seeking balance, and the balance is around the place that nature has placed man or animal or dog or bird and seeks balance and the balance is inherently a state of peacefulness. That does not mean there won't be times that aren't, but it means there is a constant desire to return to a place that is natural to the body and one might say, "Well, isn't my life natural?" and the answer for many is, "No, it isn't." It is stressed up, turned up, cranked up, bothered up, constantly through excessive sound, excessive mental activity, excessive medication, excessive, excessive, excessive. Even the toys and the business tools are very demanding of attention and they hypnotize us into believing that we will feel all right if we can operate them appropriately. We have been seduced by a system that has taken us over...it has taken us over...it has taken us over.

And John as you well know, the lessons to be taught in this are abundant, but if one is co-opted by the very system that might be the teacher, there is not sufficient space between who you are and the system itself to be able to discern that this is a classroom. Essentially, as you enter the class in this life, you become the class, or the classroom. That is not intended. The intention is that you become a student, sitting in the classroom, so to speak, independent of the classroom, independent of the teacher, independent of the teaching and get what you can as your Soul comes to learn and evolve, for anything else is to become trapped in the system itself and of course the mind loves that. It finds itself admiring itself because of the way it is trapped in a system because it values that system and has little knowledge, if any, of the role of the Soul.

You might well ask... "How can a body possibly, with a Soul and an ego, not have those communicating?" The answer to what I can see is, think not about that, for there is little evidence that the Soul and the ego communicate. They are in different places on different paths for different purposes. One of course is eternal, as we have talked about; it goes on and on and on and seeks to evolve in this process that is Divinely inspired. The other is defensive and negative and deals with "what ifs" in the very short term and passes with the body...does not go on. So they don't speak the same language. They are not for the same purpose, and in many cases they are counter-productive in dealing with each other. So think not about merging them. Allow them to be separate. Allow one also to start to rise above the other, for as we grew up, as we were acculturated into our system today the ego has predominance—the color of the car, the color of my clothes, the trim of this, all, and on and on and on—and the Soul might well ask, "What is all this about?" "I came here to school. I came here to seek my own evolution, so to speak, through this body and though I will learn and I will, I have little way to influence the ego and so I sit quietly by while the ego parades itself up and down, because that is the nature of the system that you live in.

The Druids that just came to your mind, Dear John, are an example of the opposite of that. They lived near nature (you are getting a chill...that is wonderful...thank you...ooo big chill) for they lived near nature. It was in nature that there was time. It was in nature that they connected with fundamental truths about who they were because the Soul was present. There weren't ego issues, ego demands, ego teachings, entire systems built around development and encouragement and management of the ego.

My acting life was filled with ego and I know what that is like. It is like, "Is my performance going to be good enough?" "How do I feed this?" And from that, Dear John, you have often wondered how can somebody such as myself go night after night after night after night doing the same performance. The answer is, at least in part, it satisfies the need to be accepted, the need to try to improve a presentation so that you will love me more. These are all needs related to externality and sometimes professing to be internalities (another word I have just ginned up) and yet in most cases they are not. In most cases they are almost hiding from the reality of what is—that is that the Soul is asking for space in the classroom. It is asking us to put aside this role of the short term life of the ego in favor of an understanding that there is much more, in a lot longer body...

And so the alternative view that we might speak of today, or this piece of it, is to say that while living in life requires some level of ego involvement, there is also within us this magnificent thing, the Soul, the eternal aspect of self, that has been and will be... regardless of how we treat it, present in the energetic fields of life for eternity.

To the extent that the mind can get involved, there is a choice here to honor the Soul, to speak to it, through these quiet times I mentioned, to set aside the ego's demand for attention, like a spoiled child stomping around trying to get control over things which are none of its business, and all of that, which leaves us in this enormously stuck place of a conflict between this outer world ego-demanding-spoiled-brat child approach and the wonderful quieter long body aspect of the Soul. Seeking development, seeking to bring forward into the world an offering that it brings, while absorbing from the world what the classroom has to offer, and it is much, and the Soul needs it, for its evolution requires these times on earth, so to speak, these evolutionary periods to develop, to develop, to develop.

Is it willing? Absolutely!!

Return to the Druidic period again.

Where were the demands for ego involvement in life? Almost none!

Where were the opportunities for the Soul to be in natural conditions, to be in natural balance, to develop an understanding of the relationship of an individual and its soul to nature in small communities? Complete!

They were built around the development of the Soul and its progress. They were not built around the excess of the ego.

So, I have returned almost full cycle here, Dear John, to the place of saying the reader would do well to do something I did not do a lot of and that was to find time to be alone and quiet, to explore to the extent that one can by oneself, however painful and however fearful, whatever it is that the Soul has come to do.

You might well ask, "What might trigger that discussion if you are sitting alone in some gorgeous forest and we have taken your advice?

What might open the door to any of that?

And as we have talked we have used the word "nudged" sometimes. We need listen carefully to any little event, any thought that repeats, maybe from a dream, nudges that suggest that there are areas in our life that need our attention because it is what we turn our attention to that we animate, and turning our attention to a piece of natural activity around us and watching and listening to birds for example, or swimming in the ocean, with turtles or whatever it turns out to be, has an effect on who we are deep, deep, deep within. For we are closer to nature than we believe. We are basically an animal visiting the surface of the earth as a school house, to leave and come back and leave and come back through our incarnation process. It is quite amazing…But we are not divinity; we don't have that capacity, and yet there is much in our life that acts as though we are completely guided but it requires that the free will aspect of the ego be set aside…be set aside…be set aside.

Trashed? No. For we need it to do some of our bidding, so to speak, in the earth world.

But to have our dominant aspect of life chasing or being chased by ego's desire to be better, bigger, more thoughtfully thought of—all of these sort of externalities—bigger house, bigger car, more clothes, things that have little to do with the Soul's journey through life. For the Soul matters, cares less, little about how we dress. The Soul cares little about much of the schooling that we think is important. The Soul knows why it is here and a wonderment would be to make contact with it and let it guide us, for in connecting with our Soul we connect also with many other energies. Know there is much guidance from

where I am, Dear John, as you have learned, seeking contact with each and finding it being resisted by the free-will
ego aspect of current human life for many.

So, in stepping way back, back to a place of saying
maybe I am not in charge of this and yet I have no fear of
not being in charge and letting the energies flowing
through spirit, where I am, come to you as I am, for example, as we speak right now, and ask that you open to the
magnificence of the greater life with nature, on the planet,
knowing of incarnations to come and seeing life not as this
complex, short, high tension, fifty or sixty or seventy years
but rather this being the schoolhouse we speak of that has
an eternity behind it and an eternity ahead of it as we incarnate and incarnate and incarnate over time for whatever
that means.

There is a wonder, Dear John, that we speak as we do
for my passing has led me, as you have sensed, into a different classroom, a classroom filled with the reflection on
what life was, might have been, and really is and there is
no regret, for regret suggests mistakes or other kinds of
evil-based thought. There is however an honest reflection
on what transpired and it is in that reflection that I come to

you and have asked you to spend time with me to bring this material forward as a conduit. I deeply appreciate your work. As a friend, I deeply appreciate your work. As the youngster listening to me on that little islet in the Bahamas, I appreciate your company, for you allowed the Soul to speak. There was no ego there. I was not performing for you. The weather had overtaken us; we were essentially grounded into that island with a bottle of Dubonnet, and there we were. Out came the inner part of Hume...seldom seen...and yet you recall it clearly, probably because you felt the sort of older father figure in this life on this little wind blown, rain blown island with you would have wisdom and control, etc. beyond your belief.

What you found was what we are speaking of in general here. That is that beautiful vulnerability of the human Soul as it seeks, not to control, but its passage, its evolution, its growth after incarnation, after incarnation, after incarnation, where there is nothing to dominate.

What is it that you get through domination, ego based control?

For sure you get one thing, and the lesson from this section would be that, and that is you find that you have rejected help from the world of spirit. For when the ego speaks and demands and manipulates and controls there is no space for spirit.

So, wonder not, my dear friend. It's the plight of families, the plight of the world, so to speak at the human level. It cannot be resolved until we get past the role of the ego. There need be, as we are talking here, a re-involvement of the Soul. The Soul is as natural to the human condition as the ego, but the ego is of the mind, the Soul is of the heart, and as you spoke with your grandson yesterday, it is moving from the head to the heart that is what this is all about.

Some try that by using the head to manipulate the heart and bring it forward into the world, but the authenticity is not there and we know it.

Jessie could act from the heart. I tended to act from the head and the difference was considerable in most cases. This is not a question of blame. It is a question of opening the door wider to the magnificence of what life is and what life offers us, over and over and over again, and shining the light into the notion that our consciousness need not be limited to a birth/death period. I was born and I died for it is a lot larger cycle than that and that is what of course the

Bishop speaks to you about. I am adding that here because of the importance of creating a different container for myself. As I looked at my life as ego-based, as performance-based, to cover up fear, a sense of weakness as we have talked, and yet here we are, looking at this life from another perspective, from a perspective of Soul, and as soon as one does that, one moves into a lot longer body.

So the intention here is to bring forward through these words of mine my sincere appreciation for this bigger picture. For though we as artists and poets and writers wax philosophic about all of this, there is always a question about what it really means, and rather than submitting to the notion that it is and letting it unfold, we seek to describe it in terms which in each case are highly personal and therefore inexplicable. Better we do what I am trying to do, which is to set forth a general pattern which could be thought of by many during their quiet time, that time alone, that time which I sought out in the Bahamas in Hume's Follies, where a place of magnificence, a place of nature, a place with fish and water and quiet and the "Poop Deck" as we called it...all of these sought to be places of calm, of quiet. Yet interesting as it is, though nature was more than willing, man was not and I built facilities, a lifestyle, a showplace in every case so the Cronyn's Follies were correctly named from the Soul's standpoint. From the ego's standpoint they worked perfectly. They were magnificent and yet as many have seen, including yourself, dear one, at the Bahamas, Children's Bay Cay, the complications of their operation were enormous and then containing or controlling much of the time available for their use in just maintenance and operation.

So they overwhelmed themselves through their complexity, through their mind aspect. They weren't simple the way the Bahamians lived. They were complicated the way a New Yorker lived who wanted friends to come and oooo and ahhhh, though that was never admitted to...it certainly was the case.

I think now of the beauty of all of those pursuits and I wouldn't do them differently for one moment. Yet in the context of the long-body, I have something to offer those who read and feel into this information and that is that it is easy to cover ourselves, our inferiority, our fears, our childish part with material things, be they islands or buildings and yet they are meaningless in this longer sense.

What has meaning is that we investigate who we are deeply within and seek to bring that out at whatever level and to whatever extent we can.

So, I would ask that we change the vector, if you wish. You will like that term John, the direction of our thought, not to all of a sudden become a monk and sit in a cave, for that will not work, but rather to change the direction of our thoughts such that some time is devoted to paying attention to our heart.

What is it feeling?

And to our thoughts…

What are they trying to achieve for us?

Challenging, if you wish, the ego…

Maybe ten minutes a day. I don't know…

Eastern religions have tried hard to work with this, yet they find themselves in the same muddle today that many of us are—tremendous issues around health, the constant seeking of capital wealth, damaging the soil, damaging nature in the name of something.

So the infection of the western world is running around the world, and that itself is out of balance, as you know.

So, it is at time like this that we seek inner counsel, for that counsel is connected to spirit, and let's spend one moment or two with that.

There is an infinite amount of wisdom in the world of spirit and we need to be available to receive it. The ego has no interest. The heart thrives with it for it is the Soul connected to this greater world of spirit and it is because it is of that. The ego is not of that. The ego is of the body that comes and goes. The Soul is of spirit and so it is getting closer to the Soul desires, be they modest, be they simple, be they relaxed, as expressed through an extra nap each day, a walk on the beach by yourself, holding hands with a friend that wants nothing from you and vice versa. being with animals, being in nature—not to change it but to honor it—all of these things move us back more toward that wonderful Druidic model that you so love and are writing about.

For it is in that simpler life that the fulfillment of the Soul's long-term objective is met and that "peace beyond all understanding" becomes the guiding principle for daily life, not through intention—ego based I might add—but through the fundamental truth that that is who you are deep within.

I bring this forward now because this is the first time, at this time, that I can speak in this way, through this wonderful book filled with wonderful pictures of what was based on ego in part...and we will talk more about those pictures as time goes on.

For now, Dear John, another wonderful session with you, another wonderful time for me to express myself in this greater perspective, which because of your work and your openness has allowed it to go more broadly than I suspected, moving from beyond my individual ego aspect to the larger perspective like that held by the Bishop and Eileen Garrett.

It is to you, Dear John, and Susan is here with me, that we send you our love and wish you to know of the enormous care many have for you in the world of spirit. When I speak of the world of spirit being open and caring and wishing to participate, we, you, Susan and I, Eileen, the Bishop, the Bard and Bardess and others are wonderful examples of what can happen for many, and we wish that to happen from this and your other publications.

So, carry it forward, dear friend. It is with our love that we send you forth.

Know you are being blessed and cared for.

Thank you Hume, and thank you Susan my love.
Love you both…

V

A View from Here

Hume-4 — 11/13/08, Newport Beach, California, 50:52

Good morning Hume. This is John at our beach loca-tion.

It is Thursday...I believe it is the 13th day of November.

I say good morning to you and welcome you into an-other conversation.

Good morning, Dear John, this is Hume.

Here we are at your wonderful beach.

There is so much to say and I know there have been questions about how many more of these sessions and I know that you and we will do what comes, as guided, until the information for the booklet, if you wish, is complete.

We start off the day with a theme of living with the idea that some aspect of us is immortal, for this changes much and you were wondering where today may go. The theme is Immortality.

From where we are, Dear John, much can be said as we look at life on that beautiful planet called Earth as a miracle, and you are getting a chill now, a wonderful deep chill...deep chill...deep chill, having you know that from us there is energy coming and that you as the recipient of that energy are responding. What a wonder that is, for the earthly mind that says, "How does this work, I can't see it?" and yet, Dear John, you have had many experiences, many, many, many both here at the beach we join you at, at Honaunau, on that gorgeous island in Hawaii and elsewhere, for example in Kihei where the Bishop shows up easily.

So, know this is not an illusion or delusion. It is the truth...because it is part of our story today and this part is amazingly important for it is the perception of this immortality that changes our life completely.

Know, as you will, that from our standpoint, again, as I mentioned, looking at the earth life here is beyond magnificent. Life where you are is beyond magnificent—the beauty, the physical aspects of it, the colors, the smells, the energies of it all, the beauty of it all, the highs and the lows, the wets and the dries—and on and on we go.

So, if you were a tourist coming to earth, you would say this is the most magnificent thing that could be imagined. If you were coming from a place of pure energy, and of course that is where we are, where the things that you have as you call them don't exist in that form, they are in the forms of energies and our relationship to them is very different than yours, to the tangible aspects of what you call life...from beginning to end.

So, there is much attraction for us to return at the proper timing to re-experience life on earth, for it brings forward for us great teachings. It is our schoolhouse, as we have mentioned. The schoolhouse is one of appreciating the incredible diversity of life, the incredible nature of the schoolhouse to teach about individual life, about collective life, about our relationship to nature. And above all, the fundamental truths of the long term, long-body, incarnations, repeatedly, as we have talked about, of life going on and on and on as they do and yet many, as you know, on the earth see a very small portion of this, so small that they believe that their life starts at birth and ends at death.

The book you are working on with the Bishop speaks eloquently to much of this and it arises now because part of what I need to share, what I would like to bring to the consciousness of those who read this, for many will, because of my name not because of my experience because they believe they see me as an actor and there are those who are interested in the magnificence, as they see it, the excesses, as they see it, the celebrity, as they see it, of life on earth as an actor of note and I fit the bill for them perfectly.

So there will be those who pick this book up with great interest and now find as you have that the Hume that they are reading about and hearing from is a very different Hume than the one they might have seen in the "Four Poster" or some other play. However magnificent the play was, it represented a small part of who Hume was and Hume now is in a position to see and speak and teach, if you wish, into the schoolhouse from another position altogether.

What comes today is the notion that we have constrained our view of life to the place where we live a different life because of it. More specifically, if we believe we will die tomorrow or the next day we may make decisions concerning that to bring that finality on and to think that we are closing up things that need to be dealt with. These are of the mind, all of the mind, the mind, that wonderful trap, that leads us into the smallness of who we are for it comes from a place of concern, a place of fear in some cases, certainly a place of smallness when compared with the enormity, the beauty, the magnificence of the Soul—that incredibly important part of us that resides below the surface, deep within near the heart as we like to say, which is true. For as the heart opens, the soul can speak, and as it speaks our life changes.

So part of the question for us today is…How do we get to the Soul? How do we get to this wonderful place of truth? And you are getting chills again, Dear John. For it is the opening…oooh big chills…big chills…big chills…stay with those until they have moved through and fully impregnated you with the energy of this chill. For it is in getting to know the Soul that we start to realize that aspects of us are far larger than our small mind, our small calendar of, "I'm not supposed to live more than fifty years," or, "my mother died at thirty five, so…" "What does that mean to me?" All of these interesting constraints that the mind places on life, and in constraining our lives we constrain our ability to be in life—by constraining our lives psychologically we constrain our ability to be in life.

"How then do we enjoy the beauty of what's around— the beaches, the mountains, the ocean, a clear sky, a warm day, a cool breeze, a flower, the scent of flowers, the child laughing, maybe a child crying—all of these things and more and more and more are part of the enormous mosaic that is hard to see if we are wrapped up in self, wrapped up in "me," wrapped up in a very short term life…where we have to proceed through disciplined culturally derived, culturally imposed ways of looking at our life.

And your religions, Dear John, do the same. They place enormous constraints on life, for the expectancy of any life beyond life is a story that is told in many churches, and yet how can anybody going to these churches come to that realization for the energetic experience in most cases is not there and that is the key. The key is the energetic experience of what "is" in the long-body, for this schoolhouse is bigger, has more to offer, by far, when we see it in a bigger perspective, the perspective of immortality, and the immortality isn't the physical body, as you well know, Dear John. The physical body has its limitations.

It is here to escort us through the schoolhouse. We need some way to be embodied, to enjoy, to experience, to live with the pleasures of being on the earth, to be embodied, to see, to smell, to touch, to experience the physical aspects of life and they are absolutely beyond belief—amazing, colorful, smellful (a wonderful word we can concoct for today) and on and on, for there is nothing like it in the universe. And yet isn't it interesting that they have, many have, as humans, and I had as a human on this planet, negated the very beauty, the very wonder of being in life in the first place. The schoolhouse becomes essentially a jail for many and what a wonderful waste it is of the experience of coming to life, for it is the mind that creates the jail out of the wondrous natural aspects of life.

Your work in the Druidic area is an experience that shows you the peace and beauty of the simplicity of life when one lives life on its terms, the terms of nature, that turns the schoolhouse into the wonderment of the place of joy...no, not always smooth and wonderful and smooth, but very often blissful in many respects, because it does not seek through the mind to create something different. It doesn't seek growth, it doesn't seek change, it doesn't seek, it doesn't seek. It responds to nature and in nature it finds the flow of the energies, the beautiful energies that regulate it all. For ultimately, as we have talked, we are like an animal in this enormous game called life on earth and life in spirit and that is the condition in which we live and it is in fighting to change that into something that is artificial, willfully controlled through free-will that the problems begin, and there we are, Dear John, almost back to the beginning, but not quite because the major piece of this story that's missing, as we started to say, that has to do with immortality.

Most do not believe in immortality. You may have heard it in a church, you may have read it in a book or poem or hymn, and yet there is something very real about that, for the schoolhouse that we live in—you live in, you practice in, you are receiving our messages in today—is just a piece of the energetic of all that is. As a schoolhouse, it isn't the long term body life that we speak of. It is just a piece of that, an incarnation if you wish, and there are many of them, for many as a place to grow and a place to

Often on or in the water.

learn, a place to deal with one's own shadow so that one can move forward boldly into life at all levels including the level of spirit.

So, if one views life on earth as a place of teaching, then the question might be, "What happens elsewhere?" And I am perfectly prepared to speak to that, not completely but sufficiently for the purpose of bringing the reader to a new level of thinking about the importance of their life in the longer perspective. You might call this a discussion of the "long-body" and yes, immortality and the long-body have a similarity, for immortality speaks, in my mind, to the notion that the energy field that we are, and fundamentally that is what we are, when not embodied exists in every real way, as your body does, when you are embodied. In other words you in spirit, between incarnations, are just as real, just as viable, just as intelligent in every respect, maybe more so in some cases, than if you were embodied only. And it is this incarnate or disincarnate aspect of your self, this energetic field that I am in today and many others, obviously, that is to be the source of your immortality. For when you pass from the earth plane, you pass into a series of experiences leading into this place of immortality, or a place of residing in the world of spirit, if you wish, whatever that is and wherever that is…because it is ubiquitous. When you move into this energy field which is, in a sense everywhere yet concentrated when it wishes to be, or can be, or is called to be and it is there that time passes, if you speak of time, for there is no time, and time passes and passes and passes until an incarnation comes forward and you reenter the earth plane again through a woman's womb.

So, the notion of immortality is extremely important, for the deeds that we create, that we do, that we fulfill, that we respond to in our earthly life, each time in our school, carry forward because they change the slope of the line of our own evolution. For you see, it is the evolution of the body, if you wish, the evolution actually of your Soul that seeks to be growing and growing over time and the evolution of your body is partly affected by the deeds that you do while you are in the earth world.

So coming to the earth world into this school and learning things changes the slope of your own personal Soulic evolution. So that is part of the immortal life, part of the slope of the line of the evolution of the body in the world of immortality, where you will go on and on and on and on, returning on occasion to the earth plane, those occasions being derived by energies that are beyond me to discuss. But, when they happen, you return and it is to the readers today that look at this material and the graphics that may come with it, in terms of pictures of family and maybe even some pictures, graphics of incarnation, that we seek to explain that the deeds you do, the life you lead, the connection with nature that you create and live through, is incredibly important to your entire being at the Soul level and that as you pass, and you will, you will carry that development in the schoolhouse with you. And it will be the basis of the next piece of your life in the world of spirit, as a starting point, so to speak, and as that starting point is adjusted, up or down, again, so to speak, based on your earthly experiences.

So the connections to nature, the connections to individuals, the connections to the works, if you wish, that are in balance with the energies that are you, your Soulic calling, your passion are incredibly important. For to ignore one's passion is to ignore the opportunity, amongst other things, to change the slope of the evolution of one's life as it moves into the immortal range of spirit.

That is incredibly important, dear one. You are doing graphics for the Bishop's book related to that, and we may ask that you move those graphics also into this book, for they speak of a great energetic understanding that humans need to have. And that is, I, for example, in spirit can be just as present in many respects, except the physical, in the lives of many, for we are all connected, we are all one and that just sounds like a nice piece of writing but is absolutely true. Through a thought one can bring together individuals, groups, whatever, in a way that the earthly world does not yet understand, for it fears death. It is part of the Bishop's book to try to overcome people's fear of death and I am here to testify, as Hume Cronyn, that death is not what we think it is. We think it the end of something and Dear John, as you are learning, it is just the beginning of the next stage of our immortality, for we go on and on and it is this awareness that I seek to bring at this point into life for humans, if only a hint for many. They will see Hume Cronyn, the actor that many have become aware of on the stage, actually talking, some in the first person as I am

with you, about the experience of this passage into a world
that is of spirit and, I am adding today, immortal. The
long-body, as you describe it, the long-body being a mixture of the evolutionary steps of incarnation, after incarnation after incarnation spaced by time in the world of spirit,
of spirit, of spirit.

So it is the going and coming and going and coming
and going and coming, returning again to the cyclical nature of all things. Nothing in the world of energy as you
know, Dear John, can disappear. So where did it go? The
answer is it just went out of sight. Just out of sight into the
energy field of spirit, which is right with you, next to you,
above you, below you, probably within you and yet not
seen for it is not embodied.

So there it is, this wonderful possibility, as we talk further of human beings being able to see in their life the idea
that they are immortal, that there is deep within them the
Soul. Most believe that, that passes on at the time of death
when the body is dropped and that is well understood.
What is not well understood and only hinted at by medi-
ums and other who talk about this material is that the energy is conserved, the energy of the body, the Soul, within

the body, that isn't dropped with the body moves on as though it is going somewhere. It moves out of sight—is another way to say it—and is held in this magnificently complicated very, very expanded world of spirit as an energy, and there it does what we do in this energy field. Some of us pay great attention to the earthly plane, others of us do other work, others of us help children, others of us go on and on and on. So it is an endless blending and mixture and hierarchy within the world of spirit.

Today we are focusing on the idea that we are immortal and that immortality is available and a necessary requirement of everybody's life. It is not saved especially for those of religious bent or those who practice special practices.

The realization of immortality is an incredibly important aspect of enjoying and living life, for it changes our view of who we are, even at the mental level, and the long term effect our daily decisions make on who we will become. For there is a direct connection between how we behave, if you wish, in the schoolhouse, and where we are in our line of immortality.

You might ask, can we destroy ourselves through bad decisions? The answer is no! But we can change the slope of the line of our evolution, meaning there is more to be learned, so whatever ascension may be available to us through certain kinds of activity in the earth plane, they may be unavailable at this particular time and require what you might call more work.

So, is it deadly important, or very important, that we pay great attention to our every move, so to speak, in the earth plane? The answer is yes, while being human perfection is not human and human is not perfection. Awareness that something goes on beyond the point of death, beyond the time when our physical heart stops and that that we are generally aware of is that our Soul moves into the world of spirit, based in part on how well we have dealt with the teachings that were brought to us at the earth plane.

For these teachings are real. There is an agenda that we enter the world with, that we enter this physical earth with, and the agenda is to have certain experiences. This is not a random role of dice. It is not a random connection of sperm and egg. It is deliberate.

So we are a deliberate incarnation of our own Soul at a time and location and a body and a place and a physical circumstance to maximize the possibility of us learning what our Soul needs to learn, for it is ultimately in support of the Soul's long-term evolution that we come to this earth plane to experience life.

One may say, "Well life is unfair for some as it is very different for some than others." The answer to that of course is, "It certainly appears that way." It is worth considering also what it is that individuals in life, as you put it, on the earth plane can experience and learn from those experiences that seem to be imposed on them. Consider also that they may be calling them in—there is another piece of self-will that most do not like to hear.

The notion that we "call in" our experiences in life as teachings, so we come to the schoolhouse and we sort of select the teacher who will teach us what we are here to learn. In some cases these are hard lessons, lessons that are not considered popular by the general culture, which of course is risk and pain averse even though pain in many cases is the only way to create the change for the individual, and the individual in spirit came knowing that there would be these pains and yet they were worth living through as a spirit incarnate in order that change to the long-term aspect of the Soul's evolution take place.

So, to judge what is happening on the earth plane for many, based on a judgment of what is soft, and nice and sweet and loving, may or may not be in the interest of the Soul that is having the experience. For the Soul is not the ego, not the lashing out part, not the angry part. The Soul is deep within and carries the fundamental truth of the long-body, of the eternal aspect of human being.

So, this is profound material. It is not sufficient therefore that humans continue to believe that their life starts at birth and ends at death, for nothing could be farther from the truth, Dear John. In fact it is almost the other way around. Life is continuous. Life is immortal. Life goes on and on and on. These visits to the earth plane are incredibly important for they allow exceptional growth and clearing of matters within the Soul that need to be cleared through experience. It is through the experience that we rewire ourselves, rewire our Soul's ability to deal with issues in life and the energetic fields that it is and as it changes who it is through these experiences, and it does, it is greeted as it returns to the world of spirit at a level which allows those energies that it now is to make contact in new ways with the world of spirit and move forward in its evolutionary process. For there is constant movement, constant movement forward, seeking the evolution of all toward a higher and higher aspect of self, the collective aspect of self, that is the intention behind it all for nothing is stagnant. All is in motion and all is striving, all is striving to a higher, higher, higher vibration and that vibration can only be reached through the individual's evolution and that is eternal. The evolutionary process is eternal.

Go back then to the human being and think, the next time you meet with somebody over a cup of coffee, that they are just a visitor here. What a wonderful example, and you can see it John in your mind's eye. You are sitting in a sidewalk café somewhere, maybe New York, I don't know. No, it is less complicated than that. Maybe some smaller city, maybe a foreign city, and you look at them with several eyes—one is they are a friend that you have not met for years and years and you speak to them about daily activity and what is going on with their family life and all, what movie they have seen or did they see the recent play? Or...whatever that would be.

And now you come to the realization that there is another aspect of self there also that is eternal. This self is sitting there talking about these events and yet in its longer body, it is here in the schoolhouse with you as you are and you are sharing some of your schoolhouse experience, knowing that first of all you are making an eternal connection. For that connection that you make over a cup of coffee is eternal. Interesting, isn't it, that this cobweb of connection never ceases. You leave a wire or thread with them and they leave one with you and they're connected, and yet you know that that connection will break or fail at the time of their death. That is what we are here to correct, for that is not the truth. The truth is that will never break and as they pass or as you pass, or as you both pass, that connection moves into the world of spirit with you both and it will never be broken.

So, the world of connection in the physical plane is just that.

Erase the physical part and everything else remains essentially the same. Dropping the body does not drop the energetic connections amongst all the humans involved—all the beings that come into the world of the physical plane—for it is just that the schoolhouse and the basic place of living is in the world of spirit.

And so as you look at this friend across the table for a cup of coffee you will start thinking anew. The new thought will be, "This person I am having coffee with is eternal. I am eternal. We are both visitors here. What are we doing here in these two roles? One role is the physical role of being in spirit, in life, on this planet at this time, a participant in what is, outside and yet in a schoolhouse, the evolution of our Soul. And here is another Soul doing the same thing, yet meeting the needs of their own Soul's development, and we came together."

Why you might ask, were you brought together? Because there are no accidents you know. Why were you brought together? What is it that the souls may be wishing through the connection? For these connections are important. The stories you exchange are important. It is all-important.

As you bring together friendships, as you bring together stories, as you bring together pain and suffering, all of that creates a change for the Souls involved for they are all connected as the bodies are dropped and they will be and even before they are dropped. If one passes and the other does not, the connection remains. As the second one passes the connection remains, so they are eternal, as you know from your Dear Susan. You are connected as you are finding out through our discussions together, Dear John, we are profoundly connected maybe starting as you and I have discussed from the little Islet in the Bahamas, where we both became very vulnerable. There is a wire between the two of us that looks very large to me from spirit and I remind you that though we have not seen each other for many, many, many years that connection is as real today as it was on that Islet. What a wonder that is—for immortality we will always be connected, there is no end to this Dear John, and it goes on and on and on. We may or may not meet in future incarnations but the wiring is still there.

Could we meet in new incarnations? Absolutely! Would we be playing the same parts in this play on earth? Absolutely not. They could be very different and yet fundamentally behind them all there is this understanding that the evolution of the Souls of both of us have been affected by our connection with each other and that is never forgotten. For in the world of eternity there is ultimate complexity that can manage an infinite number of connections, so to speak and it does. For it is all these energies flowing and flowing and flowing that create life, that create the incarnation of life, that support the long-body, in fact are the long-body, for that is exactly how life works.

Taking a breath here and returning, as we will, to the very substance of our discussion today Dear John, consider yourself again at the coffee table with your friend talking and now realizing that your actions on earth have the profound effect, not only on the person you are with, in a whole new way than you ever thought. And why is that? Because they are immortal also and your connection with them is affecting the energy field around them, as their "presence" with you affects your energy fields. So each contact we make is having an effect, however small, but still significant on the evolution of all those around us.

We are energy beings, fundamentally, first, last and always and it is our energetic fields that create change in others and it is our energy field that receives pushes toward changing our own energy field.

So, a good teacher, as you know, can inspire us. That is a shift in our energy field. A play that I might have acted in may have touched somebody, that has touched their energy field and vice versa. Their presence in a classroom as a teacher may affect their students. That is a shift in the energy field.

It seems complex beyond the mind's ability to understand it, and yet going back to our coffee with your friend on the Plaza "something" de la Rue or some place a fancy French name may be, I joke. Consider as you look at them or her that you are making contact with an evolutionary body that is immortal and seeing your life as you go through each step in your life that your "presence" affects others, their "presence" affects you and at the time of passage, which is ahead for all of you, is not the end of these connections. It is the beginning, if you wish, of the unseen aspect of the continuation of your life and their life and it is these energetic connections that are made to continue.

So, essentially you are whole energetically as you come into life and you are whole as you leave life and as you leave life into the world of spirit, there is a point in time again when you return, reincarnate, again whole.

People will ask, yes but... "Why does a baby act as a baby and not a Soulic adult?"...The answer is because it has the difficulty of the beginning or the opportunity of becoming a physical body and that physical body is the requirement for being in the physical plane of life. The Soul cannot be in the physical plane of life as a body, so it works with other bodies, human bodies that are here to create a body within which it can reside during its time here. There is a process of developing through the woman's womb, as you know, and through the male sperm, a new incarnation, a new body to carry an ancient Soul and this is important.

The new body carries an ancient Soul and as that body ages and grows and works in its life, does the things it does, it is adjusting the ancient Soul and as the body passes eventually the ancient Soul returns to the world of spirit.

Returning once again and maybe with too much emphasis, but I think not, sitting with your coffee friend again, there is a profound shift in our consciousness when we see everybody in our life as immortal and see ourselves as immortal. This is much of the material that the Bishop speaks to in his own way with Eileen…and yet here we are speaking to it.

If we knew our actions were affecting our future even beyond the time you call death, many would consider those activities a second or third time before acting on them.

Would one expect an immediate change by having a sense of immortality? Maybe not, but there is a profound deep understanding as that information soaks in that for many and particularly those in the second half of life—not that scampering around to find who we are part—but the part of seeking to accept and find who we are more deeply, the realization in the second half of life is not about defending against death. It is about seeing if the schoolhouse work is complete, for if it is complete the passage becomes simple. The passage becomes, for many, a blessing. It removes the struggle with the physical body, which is important for many, the endless disease issues, etc, etc of the aged and allows there to be a vision within each Soul, or within each mind, at that time of the possibility of immortality.

What is it I can do, should do, will do, am to do in support of my immortality?

A different view, Dear John, than many hold and that longer view is sobering for many and yet what a wonderment it is, because it is the truth and in that truth there is freedom, removing the descriptions of this birth/death paradigm that presently exists for many and saying, ahh yes, just a visitor into this magnificent earth world, maybe to return but certainly not with the current consciousness, for though the Soul will return the conscience maybe at some other place, at some other level, some other time.

So, the idea of enjoying and fully realizing the benefit of what this life has to offer, not struggling with it, to fight with it, to try to change it or control for that is certainly jousting with windmills, Don Quixote style, one of those mythical characters that you used to love. A nice idea, a nice myth, far better go to the windmill and blow on it to help turn the big wheel of life, however insignificant the breath might be. Intention is incredibly important, for in the world of these subtle energies of which we speak, little energy consistently applied creates enormous results. So too with the notion, fully embodied so to speak, that we are immortal and that following this passing, when it happens, how it happens and all of that is orchestrated also—that we will then be moving on into a world, that once we have left this world—is embodied also with our experiences here, for we carry our experiences here into our Soulic life, and what a wonder that is.

This is not to discipline us. It is not to shift our view of life particularly in terms of our actions on a daily basis, but the subtleness of knowing that we are creating or co-creating our own future after death is incredibly important and would change the view of many.

If a culture could understand this deeply—know that your Druidic friends did, Dear John, there are many cultures that did.

The modern culture, however, has gotten away from the notion because they believe they are all powerful in life and have no idea what happens afterward. Of course we now know, none of us are all powerful in life. We are acting because the Soul is the one that is observing and working and passing through. The ego is just a manifestation of body, protection, defense, anger, etc. and yet we have our lives wrapped around ego and as we have already discussed, that is not it. It is about the Soul.

So, we speak today to you, Dear John, about the Soul and its immortality, for it is who you are. So in these earlier discussions about getting in touch with the Soul, we are getting in touch with our immortal self and what a wonder that is, for it is the immortal self that carries the vibration of energy that brings "Peace beyond all understanding" to our body and to our current life.

It allows us to sit quietly at the beach and observe, and observe, and observe and sense our belonging here for the production of goods, for being better than somebody else, and on and on and on created by the ego out of fear is not important to the Soul. It is required for the evolution of our bodies on earth but not to be worshipped as a deity the way it is today.

As we close this I would ask that each who read it consider repeatedly in their own life at some time, be it morning or night, or at sleep or whatever, that they are immortal, that the actions they take here affect their immortality and the quality of their life and the life for many others around and that they consider how they might adjust their life with that in mind, remembering that being in service to our Soul, our deepest spirit that is embodied, that we have an opportunity to make the greatest contribution, not only to those around us but to our own life as an immortal presence in this magnificent world of energy that is connected in numerous ways with planet earth.

For now John...

For now Dear John...

We will gather again on your next schedule...

I send love, appreciation, great thank yous.

Susie is here with me.

All is well. Be not nervous about approaching these times for we radiate nothing but love to you...

And wish you to carry nothing but love forward through what is becoming a teaching we put in writing to come from the mouth of Hume Cronyn, for some may listen.

Yes we will talk more...

About the format of the book, photographs, the details.

For now Dear John, be blessed.

Hume-5 — 11/16/08, Newport Beach, California, 49:52

Good morning Hume, this is John...Sunday, a few minutes early, but there we are...a beautiful warm...Sunday Santa Ana-ish morning in Newport Beach and I welcome you...

Good morning, Dear John, this is Hume, and here we are for another one of our wonderful gatherings.

It is to you that we give great thanks, for you are bringing this material forward, as you say, from the sound of my voice which you hear, speaking it into your machines and then taking it through typewriters and what not into a place where it can be published and read by many, by many, by many, and that is as you know our intention. For there is much that I have learned since I passed and I wish to bring much of that forward, yet keep this material light enough so that many will read it. Not a tome or religious tract but something of interest, something where knowing the name of Hume Cronyn would attract attention so they can be infected by or affected by, or both, the words that come, the words that are coming to you from me, from my experiences since I passed. For much has changed. I see differently the world I lived in, not because of the world but because of me. I have changed and what I now know is, for me, more correct than what I thought I knew well when embodied, for I found that hiding behind who I was, a personality and ego, a level of development, if you wish, in the physical world was the way I really was. And yet as we have already discussed, little of that was me, for deep within me the Soul, that beautiful part of me that was relatively undiscovered, except maybe in the latter days of my life and then only glimpsingly at some event, or sometime alone, for my life was not about the Soul, as I saw it. My life was about performance, not surprising for an actor I guess, and that is the way it was to be. Nothing wrong, it is just that now it is very different for I see deep within the foundation, if you wish, on which all else was built and yet how unrecognized it was and for now it is to me to bring forward that foundation piece for each of us. For if we can each dig deeper within ourselves, we will find the magic of who we are. It is truly that, for each incarnation brings us into the schoolhouse for purpose, not just to collect things, not just to have children, not just to be somebody that we think others want us to be, but to develop our self at the Soul level for future incarnations and toward the evolution of consciousness in its greatest sense. And what greater calling could there possibly be for each of us once we get in touch with it again, for in yesteryear, your Druidic period, and others, much of what we speak about today, and over these last few gatherings, would be called "old hat," meaning there is a general awareness that that is just the way life was. However that is not what life has become, particularly in our western world. It has become a competitive, physical, non-emotional, non-heart-centered, mental, speed, domination oriented culture and consciousness. This removed us from the Soul of who we really are.

And we look at our churches, Dear John, and all of the institutions that were at one time sacred and see that few are surviving today in anything like the form or concept of their initiation many, many years ago. They have become more complicated, in a sense more dictatorial and in a sense they too have lost their way, for they have within themselves, as all organizations do, the seeds of their own demise. That is worth observing for a few minutes as we pass by this whole idea that there is salvation in our institutions, for there is none.

The institutions are the projections of man's mind into the outer world in the hopes of controlling and stultifying life to a place where there is safety, where we can feel we belong, that we know what our part is and as your daughter is finding out in her employment, it is about what goes on inside ourselves, not how the outer world treats us, that is the important. The only important thing these institutions, including the one that the Bishop was associated with, the Roman Catholic Church, have found is that though there is still a following, and a great one, that much of what it was founded on has no value today for many. It is not that the church is necessarily wrong. It is that the church and its institutions are not speaking the language which has meaning for today. They don't talk about the Soul at a depth that I wish to present. They do not bring forward a scripture that is modern enough to attract the attention of the young. They are aging and they show in each one of their joints the creakiness of age and also the accumulation of problems within their own organization.

For there is no organization, as you well know, Dear John, of any hierarchy and these hierarchies of these religious institutions are large and deep, that can survive over years without enormous change, seeking to control, and as we said stultify, or bring rules, regulations, dogma into the place of the flow of energies, the flow of energies, the flow of energies, the circulation of energy, the circulation of energy...the circulation of energy does not work, for these energies cannot be trapped. They cannot be written down and be presumed to be fixed and in this book we are working on together, Dear John, is an example. Nothing in here will be codified; nothing in here will be stultified. All will be allowed to flow and we only ask that it be held in someone's hands, and read once or twice, for that will be sufficient to open that door of questioning, to open that door of wondering, to open that door to see beyond the current dogma of society the fears death, that seeks to immortalize itself in life. And of course it can immortalize itself, but not in life. It will require what we call death, which is another form of life, of eternal life, the long-body as we have talked.

And so returning for a moment to these institutions, there are few on the planet that have survived great lengths of time, for the cycles of these institutions, like the cycle of all others, regardless of their religious basis, they do not have and can not have and can not support a message, no matter how eternal, if it is presented in a way which requires an understanding of it, a submission to it, in the great flows of nature and life as it unfolds, as it unfolds, as it unfolds. For that isn't the purpose of all of life; the purpose of life is to find where we belong in the greater flow and join it. That would be our Soul's pattern—to seek information about our Soul from outside because somebody wrote a book without the first- hand experience—and that book was written in an attempt to understand and/or dogmatize for the purpose of control, or the purpose of the collection, or for the purpose of a teaching. All of that must fail, for like the fires that are encompassing your community, there must be change. Things must be altered.

It is the cycles, the cycle, the cycle.

Returning again to the churches, even the new ones, the Mormons and others who bring forward wonderful teachings and yet they find themselves caught in the same quagmire of needing to be economically successful, of wanting to proselytize everywhere, carrying their message.

We have young people now in new youth groups seeking to find their own truth and yet they are looking for it outside of themselves. There will be no truth there. There is no truth outside of yourself that can be found or delivered by others.

You may well ask, Dear John, What about the role of teachers?

AAAhhh…good question…

There is a role for teachers if they will open themselves to truly understand who they are through the Soul seeking. Soul seeking—another buzz-word—Soul Seeking. For in Soul Seeking they will find within themselves the truth of who their "unique being" is and when we find who our "unique being" is we soon learn the teaching of it is of little use to somebody else for it is not their "unique being." Each is unique.

So the teacher that opens the door to the possibility of finding our "unique being," not through rules and regulations and books and you do this and you don't do that, but rather asking the heart and the Soul to quizzically investigate the uniqueness of who they are, how they approach life from that position, what they can contribute while they are here and what their long-body looks like, has looked like, is an enormous blessing for many for it allows many to open themselves to the great circulation of energy and therefore life and its wonderful cycles.

For it is in opening to the cycles of life, the cycles of the Soul—incarnate, disincarnate, incarnate, disincarnate—and on and on that there is growth toward the evolution of the Soul's future, whatever that is to be and for each it is unique.

There are no rules that say this is the way it is to be and if you will follow my teaching you will be this or that or something else.

So, it is the teacher that opens the door. It is the teacher that says this is possible, that at the right time we can kindle within each of us that little glimmer of hope, that little glimmer of light, that little flame that flickers, and at the right time (and it varies for each of us) we will let that flame open and open and open. It may be an event caused by illness. It may be an event of seeing a moon one day or you may be watching a plane fly or bird flap its way over the ocean for thousand upon thousands of miles…without any understanding of how it navigates.

For you see we know little and yet we try to ascribe great wisdom to our deeds and our presence.

So, in finding the Soul we also could release the need to know, for there is very little that we truly understand, and that is just as well because we would probably seek to control it if we thought we understood it, and then maybe sell it or box it or do something else.

The purpose for us individually is for the Soul to find a place to open itself to become who it is, to learn how to express, through the being that it occupies, what it came here to do, which is a journey incarnate for a limited period of time to learn, to grow, to affect others, as it will, and then to move on through this body back into pure energy and from the place of pure energy move on to the place in the spirit world where its natural home is.

So you see there is little, Dear John, that makes sense from my standpoint of organizations and particularly those that are seeking to save, salvage, redeem, individual life through organization.

And you might ask, "What do we do, because so many need to be in a place where they are guided?"

That assumption is the result of the modern world believing that there is something wrong with those who follow because we have designed a place of leaders and followers. But what if those people who are so-called followers, were left alone, not to be lead or manipulated by those who want their labor or effort on the farm or fields or on the ocean fishing, but left alone. Would they necessarily require leadership? The answer, Dear John is none at all. Each Soul comes forward with its ability to do in life what it came to do and it will. It's man's organizations that seek to gather up information, to gather up ideas, to codify as we mentioned, and seek to regulate how people live there lives, their purpose, etc, etc, etc,

So it is at this time, and there never has been a better time in life for each individual and for the planet that we honor the individual. We honor the individual Soul. We honor that each can carry its own message. It needn't be measured by whether it is in the Smithsonian Institute or wins an Academy Award. It can be measured merely by its "presence" and its willingness to fit into the cycles of its own Soul's life and development, supporting others as it can but not submitting to the will of others. Bringing forth its loving presence, receiving loving presence, adjusting as it can, as it grows, so that after this incarnation passes it moves on the wiser.

You might ask, Dear John, about sin.

There certainly is a range of activity of human beings, probably of animals also, maybe the planet itself, that speaks to a darker place.

So all is not light in this circulation, for the very nature of circulation itself requires both the light and the dark, What we seek to define would be the relative strength of these, for few, when you look at the planet, live primarily in the dark. Most live in some level of light.

Those few that find their way into the dark have found their way into a cycle through which they cannot pass but get stuck, and that stuckness is a teaching in itself for it asks that the Soul, in its stuckness, learn, learn, learn for it too is a schoolhouse. And who is to say that the activities in this dark area, which we might call the dark side, are all wrong. Maybe they carry in some cases a community energetic that needs to be expressed through deed or lack of

A day of fishing.

deed in the community and in so doing creates new balance. For if you recall John, all is in balance. The darkness
and the light are in balance, and though the human being,
the human mind, and the human Soul by and large seek
light for it is that that grows plants, it is that that warms the
air, the darkness is something that most humans fear and
yet many animals, most animals, are out and about in the
darkness of night.

So, you see we are predisposed to want to be in light, to
be enlightened, and yet our approach today to enlightenment is not to seek out the Soul's light, the Soul's path,
which in most cases leads to enlightenment. We seek out
methodologies to concretize who we are in a place to remove the fear of darkness, the fear of change, the fear of
lack of success, and all of these shadow aspects that we do
not like and yet in so doing force ourselves into the very
shadow we seek to avoid.

How does that happen? It happens by concentrating on
how to avoid something and we find out that in the world
of energy, what we seek to avoid with too much energy
becomes us, for our attention is devoted to it and anything
we devote extensive attention to finds a way of becoming

us, for that is the way it works. Know that your intention of seeking light, in a gentle way, will most likely happen because you are predisposed to it. Your intention of seeking to avoid darkness means focusing on darkness as a way of trying to avoid it. If that technique is used, darkness will certainly appear.

The institutions of the churches and religious organizations have sought to contain and control the darkness that we speak of and yet, they too start to suffer from it by trying to seek ways to control it, and that becomes the beginning of the end of many of them. Many upstart religions have sought through wonderful motivation to bring together groups of like minded people for the purpose of lightening their lives and in lightening their lives and their Souls have responded positively, until the eruption of the leadership, the control, the desire for wealth, the need to be dominant, the need to be respected, the ego aspect, if you wish, erupts into the leadership, the management, of these religious organizations and "bang" there they are looking at themselves in the mirror, seeing the very thing they sought to avoid. And when it erupts all hell breaks loose for the Soul erupts with it and says "we are not doing this" and whatever that means can often be chaotic for the person, for the leaders, and certainly for all the followers.

So, where you might ask do we go for leadership today outside of ourselves? Well let's not pass the "outside of ourselves" by too lightly. Let's first say we seek the leadership by looking within. I have said much of that and will say more of it, for that is where it ultimately is.

But on the way there, and while we are working with that, it would be useful to listen to many of the great teachers of old who wrote poetry and sometimes music, often little stories, that are enlightening from the standpoint that they open the door to self- discovery, so they are external guides to an internal process. That is the best that you can do. The secret is to avoid being conscripted into an organization which itself is caught in the light and the dark issues and seeks to provide you with answers to things that are uniquely you, and about which it has no specific understanding.

That is true, John, of all the institutions that society builds and that is why your Druidic friends in these very small communities, that knew each other well, were able to make allowance for the individual Souls within the group without seeking domination, knowing that each was there for a purpose and they would seek to exploit that purpose in a loving way within their small tribe. That works because there is honesty in the proximity of one to the other, the proximity of each to the leadership, the vulnerability of the leadership to effective leadership. In essence, if the leadership is not working, the assistant will take over, kind of thing, because they are all eating from the same bowl of soup. There is no remoteness that allows domination through control, through authority, through requirements set in paper and distributed as "the truth." For every day in these Druidic periods, and worlds of that type, there were changes that came about, some by design but many in response to nature's activities—no rain equals no harvest, we must move, fire started by lightening, we must move, wonderful food in this valley, we can stay, many new babies, we will stay, the fishing has been poor, we must move or change our fishing techniques.

And so it is that the flexibility that they had by having almost no organization and an organization very close to those it sought to organize, if at all, that it was able to be flexible and acknowledge the individuals to a high degree, not perfect, no doubt but to a degree that allowed each to express themselves, each to be heard, each to be accepted, each to be vulnerable in their own ways, and so they were.

So you see we have moved a long way from that. We have removed our government from any local responsibility. They have all delegated it upward, for fear of not being accepted in the community and not retaining the power which they are giving away by their very act, when as a city or a state one seeks federal support, no matter what the country is, one is removing oneself from the process and saying "here…you do it" and in that we make ourselves vulnerable. Through seeking to delegate upward we remove from ourselves the opportunity of having a rational local discussion that fits directly into the uniqueness of the lives of who we are.

And so, Dear John, you have always been interested in the local government—that truth is also true about local religion—for local government ultimately is the presence within you, and local religion is ultimately the presence within you, and that presence is the presence of spirit as animated through your Soul and the Soul's connection and guidance from spirit seeking to fulfill your largest calling.

What could be better then that, for it knows your uniqueness, it knows why you are here; it knows what you are about.

Why not listen to it? It is the ultimate road map!!

Why then, Hume, are so many people so lost and so caught up in all of this at this time?

Wonderful question, Dear John, for I too was part of what you are speaking of.

There is a time of cycles, if you recall, and each little flame of creative activity that sets in place a model, and you know models well, of what might be is copied. What is not copied with it is the inherent limitation of the models themselves, for there is no model without the understanding of change and models sound to many as though they are something that is rigid and you know dear well from your work—on Iona with the Druidic people, in your work in public works, elsewhere—that all is subject to change and the best we can do is to put something in place for the moment using as much vision as is available. For example, your work in wetlands, or that in Las Vegas or other places, where you were able to envision something beyond the common, and yet knowing that it is beyond the common, it's been instituted and yet it too will pass, for all is cyclical, all will be found wanting in that sense and it is only in the context of wanting something that will last forever that we are concerned about the cyclical nature of anything, for what difference does it make if it serves today. It is much like your Druidic people—there is enough food in this valley for the next year…we will stay—that speaks nothing to the following year. So too with public works and other things and all of life, medicine, religion.

Why is it that we think it will last past next year for we have no idea what next year looks like? That is a future that does not exist in the world of energy. It has not been brought together.

It has not been created, if you wish.

So, it is only in the human mind that there is some desire to think we know about the future, for fear we might not, and be a victim of what it has in mind for us, and of course that is true, for most of what we do has a short shelf life. It does not last long. My acting career would be a good example, but beyond that the career of any one play, however brilliant, has a short shelf life. Yes, we may tour with it on more than one occasion but few a generation away will even remember it, except those who are historians of the work.

It is our desire again, going back to any of these thoughts of trying to control life, to try to make it predictable so that we feel safe, and in that safety we feel there will be peace, and it turns out just the opposite for there is no peace in the creation of structure which we believe causes safety, for the structure itself imprisons us. We are imprisoned within the very structure which we believe will have us be safe.

So the price of seeking safety is everything.

So we build buildings, we create institutions, buy insurance. We do, we do, we do, we do without realizing that nobody knows about tomorrow or the day after except the Soul and yet we rush around seeking to control tomorrow...a myth...an absolute myth. Does that mean that tomorrow isn't going to be much like today for most? No, it doesn't mean that. What it means is that in the greater stretch of life, the long-body, we will be in and out of incarnations many, many, many times. We have no idea who we will be in our next incarnation, for it can be assuredly not who you are in this one, so we don't even know that, and yet it is our Soul, the deepest part of who we are, that will be there again seeking in that schoolhouse to be taught, to learn, to evolve, to seek to adjust to its long term future also, for it has that and yet it knows not what it is.

So, this Soulic energy, which is the fundamental energy of life and human life, is an amazing energy for it will be evolving, eternal. It carries its message forward. It learns, and yet it does not rely in any way on rigidity, structure. To the contrary, it relies on the flow of the energies around and in life and between lives…and in the long-body. It is amorphous, it is cyclical, it is ever changing, and yet the aggregate of it is the most amazing blessing to each human being as they find their Soul well below the ego by setting the ego aside bit by bit by bit, to a final place where there will be time to get in touch with who we are. At that time the need for structure, the need for leadership, the need for religion, the codified sense of it will disappear. We can sit on the beach, for example, and feel absolutely free and what else could there be? We could be in an airplane flying across the continent, look out the window and feel abso-lutely blessed by a presence we know not of, and yet here we are doing something magnificent in a magnificent place, without the need for an idea of how all this comes about, for we will never know that, that is not the human condition, it is not the condition of the Soul. The Soul's mission is clear. The schoolhouse concept is clear, but the idea of our mind and our ego grasping it all, seeking to concretizing it and write something about it so we can sell something or become greater, is an elusion, for we already are that greatness. We are that piece of the Divine plan that lives and loves and sees and what is being asked here as I look back is that we open to the greatness of who we are, not out of fear, not out of hoping people will accept us, but out of a deep knowing that there is a fundamental truth within each of us, within each of us, no matter who we are, where we are, what we are, that seeks expression, that seeks to contribute, that seeks to make itself heard and known and carries its message forward. For that message is eternal, that message is blessed. The message can enjoy what is in life, for each incarnation is chosen methodically for the purpose of being the schoolhouse for those seeking entry into the earth plane at this time and there are many, for they can see the myth that has been perpetrated in the name of control, the name of ego, the name of domination. Governments have gotten larger than religion...can you imagine that?

Think about that, Dear John, that the governments of the world are larger than the religions of the world in many respects. What a strange thing, for the religions started out to be closer to the Soul and the governments were never about the Soul. They are about domination in the name of organization, efficiency, and public service, and yet they have turned their eye away from that to self- aggrandizement and self-perpetuation. Nothing to do with public service, though there is some of that, and for those who work within them, many give their lives to that, artificially, without understanding, that the intention of government is its own future at this point.

Going back to your Druidic model, nobody with your little tribe would have survived even hours in a leadership position if they said, "this is all about attending to me" and yet if you take that model and blow it up into the world today, that is exactly where we are. The big governments are interested in their own future and collaborate with big business and there is nothing wrong with either in its proper perspective. The individuals they seek to serve or control, however, get lost and are lost and are hurting and I see that.

And so I write through you, Dear John, through my name, the Hume Cronyn name, to bring forward messages and there may be more than one, asking people to get in touch with who they are within, deeply, for there is where divinity is, there is where personal counsel is, there is where health and happiness are. There is no other place— moments here and there maybe. Lasting? No, and the contribution they make to their own evolution by moving past the notion that there is salvation outside of oneself, for all of what we speak of is a myth, and if they turn inward even a little bit, they start to open the door to the magnificence of who they are, their own divinity and will start turning their back toward the government and even most religious teachings that don't honor and open the door to their Soul. For that is the work of today—to move inward, to find out who each is and notice how we respond to the world around us and in noticing that eliminate those things that are interfering with the flow of who we are.

It takes bravery, it takes courage, it takes a willingness to stand apart, such as yourself, Dear John, from those that would seek to control, from those who set the standards…from those who tell us whether we are right or wrong or healthy or unhealthy or nice or not nice or friendly or not friendly or belong or don't belong, for you do belong. Each of you that may hear or see or read this belongs—be there no doubt of that—belongs in every respect…to the world in which you were born, for your Soul has come, has chosen the body, has chosen the family, has chosen who you are in your life and guides (with the exception of what the ego dominates over) and guides the development within the schoolhouse. Recall the ego's activities, directed through its individual self-will can cause havoc with all of this; can have us at the right church at the right time to hear hollow preachings that mean nothing to our Soul. On occasion that same ego may find us in a church, as you did in Germany, in tears…not because you understood the words of the preaching, but the combination of the music, the possibility of your Bishop father being there or being in a place like that, opened your heart wide, and you can feel that right now, Dear John, for it is opening the heart that gets to the Soul for that is where the Soul lives. And so you get this chill, chill, chill, the chill of being in that church in Germany, the chill of feeling an open heart, the chill of now knowing that it is also the Soul's presence coming forward through the heart.

You have often said that the edifices of these large institutions called churches are THE magnificent aspect of the church itself, and there is reason for that. As you have learned, the geometry of these incredible buildings and places has a divine inspiration behind it and your heart and Soul know that, for their divinity sees within those buildings divinity itself. That alone, as you move into a church, or into a magnificent valley, or into a grove of trees resonates with the Soul and the Soul reacts, in your case with tears. Those are tears not of distress. Those are tears of absolute joy, of the wonder of being present for speaking time, for hearing time, for listening time, for seeing time in a location where the Soul is open and the Divine speaks.

It is that simple, Dear John. Bring yourself into contact with opportunities when the heart can open, and when it does we know it and it is to that that we need to place our attention and honor these opportunities, for they are all around and so are some teachers who speak not of the dogma but speak of the opportunity, through reading, writing, music, singing, dance, color. All of these things are energetics. All of these can create change within. All of these can pare away the obstacles to the discovery of the Soul. For those who love dance, they speak of the time of euphoria related to dance as they do it, and that euphoria, Dear John, is a connection of the heart to the Soul. It is the passion you have been praying over recently. Getting in touch with one's passion and knowing that being in touch with one's passion that life, the influx of divine energy, transforms all into a place of great wonder and love and peace. And what more could one speak of, as one approaches life, than peace—peace from lack of structure, peace from lack of dogma, peace from lack of religious protocol that seeks to subordinate self to its teachings.

It is through this writing, through you, Dear John, that I trust this message will be heard and read, for it is simple and profoundly complicated. For as one is raised in this mechanical business, intellectual world, control, rules, regulations and on and on, one realizes how far away one is from your little tribe in the Druidic land of Scotland and it is by keeping that Druidic land of Scotland alive in each individual body and mind, for each that may read this has a location in their history and their Soulic history that is much like that tribal land, whether it is an American Indian or in Mexico or other places around the world.

Think not of how we can aggrandize ourselves and these systems or improve them and fix them. Think personally, personally, personally about leaving space in our own lives to move away from all of them for an hour, for two hours, for three hours—it makes no difference—but to commit time to realize that you need none of these structures to be who you are and the new who-you-are which is really the old who-you-are deep within will find a way to bless all of what is as it finds its freedom to express itself fully in life, through an open heart, and love.

For this open heart and love does not judge. It doesn't compare. It doesn't seek to control. It just "is" in its fullest sense, an aspect of the divinity, in its wonderful circulation of energies you know as life that has blessed you and many others, including myself, to be embodied on the planet and what a magnificent journey that was, and has been, and is for you.

So, let us close today with a sense that this is a preaching, if you wish, about freeing the Soul to be who it is, and recognizing that the institutions, no matter how highly vaunted, or how aged, or how wisdom oriented they appear to be, interfere with the flow of the Soul and it is our job only to set aside time to be quiet, however fearful that may be for us, to open ourselves, open ourselves, open ourselves, Dear John, as you know, to what the heart and therefore the Soul wish to show us.

And we will find HEAVEN ON EARTH...HEAVEN ON EARTH...HEAVEN ON EARTH.

My blessings to you, my friend...

We send our love...

We thank you...

Blessings, blessings, blessings, Dear John.

VI

The Blessings of This View
for Others

Hume-6 — 11/19/08, Newport Beach, California, 55:06

Good morning, Dear Hume.

It is November 19, a few minutes after our nine o'clock time, about nine fifteen.

And I welcome you to the beach again, the location of our communications, this being our sixth gathering.

Good morning, Dear John, this is Hume. It is a wonder all of this, is it not? That you and I can speak through no medium at all, no wires, no hook-up lines, no nothing...spirit to body...quite something, Dear John.

We are now well into the material for this book. The photos of course will come. Some minor editing will be needed and yet it seems as you have thought, it is wise to leave this as a discussion between the two of us as the format.

For to try to edit it toward a speech, or some such, could easily destroy the flow and in that bring the whole book into question, for it is easier for you to be a participant here, with your name on the book also, and eliminate the questions about what you are doing here. Your role is built into these very communications and that has to be accepted as it is for that is how it is. So we move forward on that premise or those premises and what a joy this is, for I feel that much of what needs to be brought forward has been brought forward, and yet pieces here and there will need to be polished up and added to.

There is the very human aspect of all of this that we can address today, for it is the human being, the being struggling to be in life, struggling to try to do things correctly, trying to be an adequate lover, spouse, mother, father, parent, teacher, and on and on.

For we have complicated life to a place where we judge, we judge, we judge.

And when do we get the freedom to be ourselves?

When do we get the freedom to be in nature, our sister or brother in very real ways, and relax into "what is"? For the majesty of life, and it is majestic, is lost as the mind takes control and seeks to discipline us for its purpose, its ego-based purpose, to control, to regulate, to introduce and use free will to thwart the very flow of the body, the Soul, the heart as it seeks freedom.

And so it is to the human being today that I wish to speak for a moment and ask some penetrating questions, the most penetrating of which is: Why would we submit to a life of discipline coming from outside, if the choice were given?

The alternative is to go inside, as I have mentioned on a number of occasions, and listen to the magnificence of who we are there. If we were to trust that the inside had the information, has the beauty, has the long term interest, is connected to the Soul, and that the Soul is real.

For the culture has not focused inward. It is focused outward, and in doing that, it has abandoned its greatest resource.

It seeks ways to reclaim comfort in ways that satisfy external feelings, external sound, external food, external everything, when merely believing in and turning inward to be who we are, to be our own Divine presence that we are in relationship to others, in relationship to a tree, the beach, a dog, nature, where we vibrate in sync with life and not find ourselves at odds with life.

For few, if asked today, would say they are really enjoying their life. Still fewer would agree that they are fulfilled by what their life means to them.

Something is missing and it stands right before them, but they look past it because the culture has moved away from your Druidic friend's culture that spoke to the simplicity of life and the primacy of self, not overriding the small community but always within and around and felt through the land and through animals, through their idea of gods. All of that allowed a simplicity, an understanding of, a connection with primal times, and we are primal animals thinking something else because the mind has directed us outward.

How then does one seek to separate oneself from the treadmill of this current culture, for it is doomed on its current path?

Just consider the idea that growth continues on and on and on. We all understand at many levels, once we consider it, that growth can not continue and yet these systems which are all wonderful and provided for many though they require growth, or they believe they require growth, to the place, without examining the long term future, that is bound to cause the collapse of exactly what they are.

And isn't that the very aspect of all cycles?

The cycles lead to their own collapse and reversal, so to speak, though in nature they are natural and flow one out of the other without distress. For humankind, however, the mind tries to control, pushes things beyond limits and therefore when the reversals come, they become far more serious to the individuals involved, cataclysmic in some cases, for change moves hard, uneasily for humans, for they try to lock in control, prevent change in the flow of life on a day-to-day basis in the hopes of security. As we have discussed, the security does not exist in trying to concretize the outside world, for it will not be held in place. It is not the nature of Nature to hold anything in place.

The beauty of the flow of Nature, the cycles, life, as it has been delivered to all of us as a gift, is that if we will float into it like riding on the ocean, the waves may get a little bit higher or lower or from left to right or front to back, but as we float on them we float with them. We are not seeking to stop the waves, not seeking to change their direction. We are just acknowledging that it is and we are part of it.

That too is true with life. The difficulty is that man has created reason to fear, to try to manipulate the ocean, in this metaphor, to control the height of its waves, to change the frequency of the waves and on and on to the place of trying to have a level flat pond and that as you know, Dear John, is not what life is about at all. The very nature of Nature brings extremes, brings highs and lows, brings cycles, and that is its great beauty. It is as you know also the beauty of riding with those cycles, accepting them for exactly what they are, and that is the uncontrollable aspects of nature of which humans are a small part, not as their mind might say, a dominant part.

It is not for us, for you or any other generation to take Nature on in some way which will formally cause a schism, and yet you are headed in that direction. As the land is abused through overuse, as the food quality drops through mass production, as the use of more and more pesticides, insecticides and the like are used to try to control crops being attacked by animals, bugs and things of this type, so in a sense there is a degradation of the food supply and a poisoning of all associated with magnificence of the control of vermin and pests and bugs and things, for the short term gain has certainly been there. The tonnage is up and on we go.

But behind this is a growth in population and a belief in the system that says "every thing must grow" and the notion of this material world we live in as the objective of life.

As we propounded here over several of these sessions, life is not about trying to carry the present systems to their extreme. To the contrary, it is the intention of life to be a schoolhouse for the Soul of each individual and there is no need for these schoolhouses to be threatened and taunted, burnt down if you wish, through man's aggressiveness about why he is here, through fear of leaving, through fear that he means nothing, all owing to the absence of a meaningful relationship with his Soul, for the Soul knows why he is here. The Soul is part of the schoolhouse process; something is to be learnt here.

And so I would ask the people listening, reading to direct their attention once again to:

What is it that the schoolhouse is offering and asking?

What is it that their Soul, deep within, is yearning to experience?

What is it they are ignoring deliberately in an attempt to have smooth relationships with people that they have nothing in common with?

What is it that they are trying to accomplish in fighting with Nature over land, over spaces for growing things, over population increases, and on and on? For we don't listen to nature and it is now time to do that.

So, again returning to the fundamental idea of paying attention to the Soul's journey:

What is it here to do?

And you might ask: How do I find that out?

The answer is, you listen to yourself...those small quiet nudges we have spoken of, where from within we get a sense of—how about over here or how about there—or other little nudges and nudges and nudges that are our inside voice speaking to us and asking us to be responsible and responsive to it in its own quiet way.

And you might say, Why doesn't it, if it is such a powerful voice, dominate our life? And the answer is because it cannot compete with the ego if the ego chooses to use free-will to kibosh the inner notions that come forward from the Soul.

So the soul that is ever-lasting culture or long-term piece of who we are in the long-body gets set aside very easily in a culture that is all externally oriented. Again, your Druidic folks sitting by the fire and quietly working the fields, in "being" as opposed to "doing," were seldom confronted with the obstacles of how to not listen to the internal because their guidance, much as the American Indian and many others, was about listening to the wind, listening to the birds, listening to the internal guidance. And John you recall listening to the birds in Honaunau when you knew one day that as you connected with spirit, the birds were chirping in a tree right next door as though in your ear, as if to celebrate your connection and you can feel that now in your heart and your Soul, for there is a hitch in your voice now as we move together in this process for the wonder of how Nature knows what we are doing, the wisdom that is there and how tiring it must be for animal life to watch us be who we are. For the very beauty of what life has to offer, many are passing by in favor of constructs, of businesses, of religions that we have spoken of. Money systems, of bartering systems, all aimed at "things" and growth on the assumption that those two will lead somewhere in life.

And how many, Dear John, are you aware of that as they get to the time of earthly passing look around and say, "Ahhh, if I only had that new car. Ahhh, if I only had the new house, etc, etc?"

It doesn't seem that way does it, Dear John?

To the contrary, it seems that most of these things that we pursue with such vigor have little meaning. It is the peace that comes when the Soul starts to move forward in this passing process that the mind has let go and it is finally an example of where the ego is detached and we start to see in that moment before death a person in touch with their Soul, living their Soul, and in doing that find themselves at peace with life and many times for the first time in their life and realizing the beauty of all that is and was. And many at that time could happily recreate their lives along a different model if there was anything in the culture to support it.

So, if this book is about nothing else, it is about finding deep within ourselves, through listening to ourselves, and by the way please know that voices are forever speaking. They speak and speak and speak and are ready at any time to come forward, whether it is through dream, whether it is through a hunch, whether it is through guidance that seems to come from somebody else's voice, whether it seems to be "out of the mouth of babes" as they say, it makes no difference. It's moving away from the outer world of definition of who we are to an inner world, making notes, keeping a log or daily writing. All sorts of techniques are available if we were to pursue them and do pursue them persistently, as you have, Dear John. You find change takes place, for it wants to take place...it wants to take us back, more toward the Druidic culture.

Does that mean abandoning all the modern life and everything that comes with it? No! It does mean modulating it to the place where it does not dominate our life as the objective, where we spend ten or fifteen years or twenty years of our life dedicated to essentially the accumulation of housing and wealth and cars, in the name of trying to fit in with society's judgment about who we are, for these things matter not, they matter not to our children.

You came, Dear John, from a place of little wealth and does that ever affect you?

Yes...positively! And you feel that right now in your voice.

For it never had an effect on you to drive you into a place of dedication to the accumulation of wealth. For the accumulation of wealth and housing and all in response to poverty comes from a place of fear, trying to prevent what was from repeating itself.

Know, Dear John, if it is to be repeated, Nature and your Soul will repeat it. If, as in your case, it's to be a humble place of beginning to be used throughout your life to guide you, to let you know that you do not need to proceed toward great wealth because you lived without it, you are not fearful of being poor because you understand what it is about. You were most loved in times when you were poor, not the only times you have been loved, but you were loved heavily during those times.

So we see that much of what we do is in defense of who we feel we AREN'T.

That is of course because we have not gotten in touch with who we are.

The notions here are simple. It is my experience since I passed to look at where I have been, what has gone on in my life on earth, realize, as I have mentioned, how much of it was in pursuit of the "golden ring" where I would be O.K., where Hume could be what he dreamed he might be, listening to the outer world to judge who he might be rather than turning within. Though there are those glimpses, they were not dominant. My life was in pursuit of a person called Hume Cronyn and image called Hume Cronyn, a popularity called Hume Cronyn, and so it was.

But so it is not now, and I bring this book and material forward with the absolute intention of speaking to many that may pick it up, again as I have mentioned, because of the name and wonder...

What does he have to say now?

What kind of strange communication is this?

So you, Dear John, and I are connected in this "strange" form of communication which as you know is called channeling and your work with me, and thank you for that, to bring forward a new view of who I was and could have been, more comfortable, more at peace with myself, more in sync with my Soul and its development, more in sync with the schoolhouse. Yet the schoolhouse idea works, for it is through the schoolhouse that I lived my life and it is from the schoolhouse that I graduated sufficiently to decide to come back to talk to you and reflect on what had gone on. So somehow in the schoolhouse I learnt that there is more to life than the way I proceeded in the schoolhouse and so by contrast I have something which I believe is important to offer to those that are prepared to hear it, and that is that "they are what is within" and what is without is less and less important, even in the culture where it is deemed to be the Holy Grail. It is not that what is within is Holy, it is Godly, it is Divine, it is asking all the while that its experiences be listened to, that its guidance be listened to, for it is the fundamental aspect of who we are. The body is not. The body is the vehicle for being here in this most magnificent place and when we are in sync with our Soul the wonder of being here at all, the wonder of each flower, the smell of each flower, the growth of roots, the ripples in the sea, the winds, fire, the moon, looking at planets, all magnificent and beyond us in terms of control at every level, each with their own wisdom, incredible wisdom built over thousands of years. Recall we only live a little tiny time in each one of these times on earth.

Many trees, as you know, Dear John, are hundreds of years old, many generations in our lives, and yet we chop them down as though they are insignificant. They carry wisdom, as you know, because you have talked to them and they see the difference and the similarities amongst us all. They are wise. What they lack is the mobility that we as humans have, and that mobility makes us wonderful, capable of many, many things both good and bad.

It is now a time to consider, where from here? If one were to try to summarize what is here, what would one say?

I say simply that I seek your attention, dear reader, and ask that you sit quietly with this book in your lap or hold it in your hands and as you do, Dear Reader, breathe deeply and ask, How is it that you can attend more to the stirrings of the Soul? And see what comes.

It might be a picture of you with a pencil in your hand, writing on a pad.

It might be someone such as you walking on the beach.

It might be you tending to an animal.

But capture the glimpse and note it for it is through these little nudgings that a new picture is created in your mind, not new to the Soul, but new to the objective aspect of your mind thinking about it.

And as these ideas, these nudges, accumulate, follow through on each.

Often a day or two will go by when we feel very Holy and we will try to do what has been asked, or what feels right, but then we soon drop it in favor of being too busy, doing something in the outer world that somehow fits into the puzzle of how we fit into the outer world or wish we were in it.

So we have to constantly refer ourselves back, day after day after day to the wonderment of who is and what is within and it is devotion to that that is guaranteed to bring forward, yes, guaranteed to bring forward a sense of direction, a sense of interest, a sense of excitement, even for those of us that are older, or tired, or maybe even not well. For these energies within transcend the body and in that transcendence can bring to the body, independent of the body's traumas, energy, thought, feelings, encouragement, almost a youthful sense of commitment to something greater than what the ego might say is the self, for the ego knows not of the self. The self is of the Soul, that deep part, the real part.

Why do this at all, one might ask?

There are many answers to that. Some are philosophical; some are sort of more businessy. Some may have to do with family lineage. Maybe the greatest and loftiest is to be of service to God for the gifts of life, for the gift of the Soul coming to the schoolhouse, for the opportunity, at all, of being in life, for that alone is a wondrous experience beyond your imagination and yet how simple it is to never consider it and take it all for granted, just because you are here, you are here and that is the end of that.

But this aspect asks us to step back, way back, and think about what it takes to bring us into life, the unknown processes and particularly the incarnation and the immortality aspects of the Soul. What an amazing series of events have to take place. They are inexplicable in man's mind and maybe some day will be understood.

It is easier to see the reproduction of the body through birth and death and birth and death and birth and death; less easy to see the immortality of the Soul selectively moving into embryos for the purpose of the Soul having the experience and directing and guiding the experience of that incarnation of the body.

So the highest level is honoring the gift of the gods that we have life at all and that this life, manifest life on the planet is to be used to its fullest and the fullest is defined by the Soul and the Divine, and not the local community store or business or place of competition, and systems designed to prevent us from being who we are in that they so totally distract us through their cultural control that many have never even heard the word Soul, except in a piece of poetry and it has no meaning in their current life.

Another reason to pursue this is to honor the contribution the Soul has made to our life and for us to seek to contribute to it and its evolution into the future, as it is immortal. So to the extent that it has served us, we seek to serve it, and that is an amazing, amazing profound thought.

A third strong reason to be interested and committed, beyond the evolution of our Soul, is the physical aspect of the body to body to body connection, which is what most people believe is all of what life is about, for the Soul and its evolution of coming and going is not understood and known by many. However this book may change that.

It is to our children and our grandchildren that we may look and say…

What would happen if they knew also, through us, the wonder of the Soul and its role in our lives and we pass that on to set a new standard for our children and our grandchildren, and by the way, the grandchildren are noticeably affected by their grandparents for they carry the wisdom, the quieter wisdom that comes with age.

But what would happen if we brought to our children and grandchildren the notion of what we speak of and imbued them with the idea that their life need not be solely dedicated to the culture of competition and "things" and that within they housed in every real way their own Soul that has incarnated into their life for the purpose of being in the schoolhouse with them? Changing the model essentially of what we hand down intergenerationally, parent to child, parent to child, parent to child, so there becomes a cultural shift possible for those that are able to grasp what we are speaking of and many will.

The fourth reason, and I am sure there are many others, that seems important from where I am today in the world of spirit, is to honor on behalf of the transitioned ones the ones that came before the immortality of all these Souls. To honor that, through paying attention to the processes that we speak of, of listening to the nudges, of paying attention to the guidance that comes, for there are many transitioned ones who wish to speak, who wish to be heard, who have wisdom beyond belief, who can't wait to see the acceptance and judgment adjusted through the use of its guidance. Not to dominate mankind, but to observe and to underscore the opportunities made available Soul by Soul by Soul or person by person by person to add to this wonderful mix of life, this Divine mix of life, of incarnation after incarnation after incarnation, the complications of which are unbelievable in terms of trying to understand it all. But the bottom line for them is to see and feel being honored, not that rave notices are required for those that are transitioned, but the angels do smile, the spirits do applaud adjustments in human behavior toward the higher goals of the evolution of human kind and this is profound, profound, profound.

So, one's life following these four might be driven in new directions toward working with the inner noise of the Soul, the inner sounds of the Soul, the inner guidance, hearing the guidance from the transitioned ones, and I am an example of that and there are many, many others that nudge.

Even your wonderful pendulum, Dear John, provides much, but to see yourself as a contribution to the evolution of humankind, to see yourself as part of the evolution of humankind and the contribution you might make and can make and your Soul wishes you to make on behalf of your Soul's commitment and aspect of this greater, greater, greater whole.

One can feel very humble as one approaches life as a servant to the greater evolution of humankind and one might say that "I'm not important" as a president or a military leader or something that is important and there, Dear John, many need to learn that it is the Soul's progress that is important. Their physical standing in the earth plane and what block they live in and what community they live in, whether they are president or not, though it may affect their own transition, really is not important. Important is the honest connection with the Soul. Living life through their soul and enhancing the evolution of their Soul and through that the evolution of the Souls of humankind.

So, worry not about status; that is of the ego. Worry not about working hard to prove something; that is usually of the ego. Connect with the magnificence of life, whether it is an ant, a snail, a tree, a mother, a new baby, a rabbit, an elephant, a rhinoceros, of courseerous, a little joke.

For the human standards as we have discussed are not the standards for your contribution. The standards of your contribution lie in assisting the Soul and its progress and seeking to elevate its progress in the schoolhouse through each and every incarnation and all the while passing on to the children, to the other generations and maybe to those around you quietly, not as a preacher, but just as a living light, for that living light is seen by many and responded to by many, not to create change or demand something from them but a reflection of what can be. For each, though concerned from the standpoint of their ego's condemnation of themselves, that they may not be worthy of what others

The Bahamas, a second home.

have, there is no such judgment in the world of spirit. All are worthy, all are worthy, all are worthy. Of what? Of fulfillment through connection to the Soul, through fulfillment which turns this life, on earth, as I have mentioned before, into heaven on earth.

From the things that cause friction, that take our energy, that remove our focus from who we are and how we can contribute to the outer world of who they are and what they are doing, we move to become real, real as defined from the blessings of being in life, the blessings of carrying the Soul of enormous wisdom, the blessings of being an immortal part of the Soul life, the blessings of biologically being able to recreate for those that are chosen to do that, and the blessings also of passing our message along to our children through our deeds and actions and beliefs. Far more important than sending them off to school or to church or some religious circumstance, for they learn by who we are, what we speak of and what is important to us. Though when they are young they may not respond immediately, as they age they will see the wisdom of the wisdom of the wisdom and decisions will be made which will affect the culture they live in, all of which affect the evolution of the Souls of many and in so doing affect the evolution of humankind to a higher and higher calling.

It may seem strange that Hume Cronyn comes forward, an actor, yes, well known, well decorated one might say to speak of the Soul and the heart and the difference between the cultural view and our inner view and yet why not? Voices need be heard to bring forward these truths, for it is in these truths that the future lies. It is in these truths that the Druidic period lasted for hundreds and hundreds of years. Nature will always be changing. The world of spirit will always be changing. The cycles will always be cycling, and yet we here, now have an opportunity of seeing where the results of the material aspects of life have lead and it has deflected us away from the Druidic model, and that is fine. However, it overshot in its cycling to a model where an individual deep within is of little importance.

So, Hume comes forward as I am in speaking with you, Dear John, to point out what is learnt from the world of spirit by looking at self, self examination of my own life, my own deeds, my family and on and on, and from this world of Transitioned Ones seeing that the alternatives are at hand, just barely covered by a thin veil that, once penetrated, could change life for many, many, many and could in fact be one of the answers to the enormous shifts in life that the cycles of the planet require. For shifts there will be, beyond what most imagine and as one reaches down to find out who is within during these times of great trauma, one will find that the outer systems of governance, of religion, and more business finally mean nothing for they collapse first and we stand in a mirror, before a mirror looking at ourselves at that time and ask...

Who are we?

What is this about?

And through practice, through bringing our Soul forward, we find we know what it is about. It is about cycles of life. We are in fact a cycle of life through our Soul's work and through our body's work. We can say we are a part of all of this; it is part of us.

We still have our work to do, our Soul's work to do, whatever that passionate calling is within, and there we are, not relying on the outside world to hold us as a mother might. Relying on our Soul and our information about the inside world to provide peace and comfort and define our connection to life around us in nature, the natural processes of this enormous planet, the glorious cycles that we live in.

So, in our little boat on the great ocean we will ride the waves with enormous understanding, deep within, that it is not a question of flattening the sea, for that cannot be done. It is a question of having enough wisdom to operate our internal boat to ride the waves as given by God to all of us as a gift beyond belief.

I close then today by referring back to these four reasons, by turning inward is a wonderment, a service to you, a service to your family, a service to the community in the long run, to all of life, to the Transitioned Ones, and to the Divine however you define that.

It is with great love that I send this message, heartfelt, to all that read this book and to you, Dear John, and to my family, for it is a great gift also to them and their children, for it may seek to put in perspective in a new way all that celebrity may mean in their family line and the wonder that it came from, that came from it as the cycle, within the family line, swings back to the guidance of Transitioned Ones in spirit, to deep work within.

I send my blessings to all...

JOHN—*Thank you Hume...*

HUME—You are very welcome and the thank yous are to you, Dear John.

JOHN—*Should we be meeting for the seventh session?*

HUME—I think that would be good for we can look at briefly in that session the next sort of physical steps, with family and beyond, and if there are loose ends we can pick those up at that time, though I feel quite complete.

And though we may have exceeded the page count, that is of no account.

And I think, Dear John, assuming a little editing of this work, not from a standpoint of arrogance about its quality, but that its energy be retained and that you are not burdened with the idea of trying to create new images, new thoughts, new feelings for the flow of what we have discussed. It also allows the reader to understand that there was a discussion of a sort, though primarily a monolog and puts a frame of reference around the proceedings, how this works in publication we will have to think about later.

I leave you now with wonderful blessings and thank you, thank you, thank you.

Again, Dear Susie is here and she is blowing you a kiss.

You are to connect soon in new ways.

We honor your vulnerability.

We honor the clarity with which you carry through your conduit the words that come forward.

Much love for now…

VII

The Longer View

Hume-7 — 11/23/08, Newport Beach, California, 52:57

Good morning, Dear Hume.

This is John.

This is our seventh gathering. I welcome you to this beach location where we have been before. It is early on Sunday morning.

I welcome you.

I did bring a list of all sort of possible odds and ends that I could think of, some of which you may be interested in, some of which you may just wish me to take care of.

So, I open the floor for what is to be the discussion for today.

Good morning, Dear John, this is Hume…slight overcast I see, and yet what wonder it is that we have worked together to bring forward this marvelous story, which is as

I see it from where I am is majestic, majestic in that it is magical also, beyond belief.

For many will wonder, how could this have possibly happened?

And you and I will know, because it happened from deep, deep within, within both of us, within each of us, as we opened to what is our truth, our desire to be of service, our love of life, and the wonder of all of this, including this gorgeous planet on which you physically ride at this time, near this beautiful beach.

So, we move now toward the end of these several discussions and I wish to bring forward a few more points before we work with your list.

Life for many is quite difficult for they have placed themselves in a position of seeking to manipulate and manage the outer world, the world outside of themselves, the world of money, the world of schedule, the world of performance, the world of appearing to be something which we may or may not be. And the commitment to that is, as we have talked, putting us into a cul-de-sac, that term you love so much. And the cul-de-sac is a place at the end of the street—essentially it goes nowhere. For in the longer term, those issues have little to do with the evolution of the Soul, that deep part within that seeks to grow in this wonderful schoolhouse. It seeks to learn from the experiences of life. It seeks and seeks and seeks and in that seeking enriches your life, the life of each of us, more and more and more. Because one of my experiences, that of a failure to dig deep within, left me often in the cul-de-sac and as I now see it that was a waste of my time and energies because it was insincere in a sense of what the deepest part within me wished to have happen, wanted to have happen.

I was caught essentially in a micro-culture, a culture of high-level performance, of high-level expectation, of high-level reward and all of that seemed well worth it. For at the time, I was unconscious of the sacrifice being made by entering that cul-de-sac with its bright lights, and bands playing, its marches and all the wonder of it all.

For what was missed is what we have discussed and that is the deep search within for the Soul, and as the Soul finds its path in this wonderful schoolhouse and if one focuses, as I suggest one does, on this long, long-body of many incarnations one realizes that there is a different view to be taken of all of this.

So let me emphasize at this point, Dear John, the view. The most successful view for the long-term body of life is almost that of a transitioned one. No, you needn't die to be able see this. But if you were each day to move yourself to a place of a longer view of life, where you see several incarnations of the Soul, knowing that the body of each incarnation is dropped and doesn't continue on but the Soul does. And if one sees one's own Soul as incarnating and incarnating one might then be willing to accept the notion of the schoolhouse, for why else would we be brought here. The bulk of our time, which of course does not exist, is in the world of spirit, is in the non-physical realm, and many wish to come to the physical realm for the experiences.

So it is in the experience in the physical realm where the schoolhouse is and if one can look at the schoolhouse, much as one might when raising one's children, that the school is an important aspect of our trip through the millennia.

And so, if we could look at life from the standpoint of, "What is it that it appears I have been brought here to learn?

How can I go about learning it?

What is it I can contribute to life which will support my experiences here in a way that, when I leave, two things have happened...

One is that I have met many of my Soul's goals for being here and secondly, I have been of service to humankind in a way that is meaningful to all that are here, either in Soul or in body."

So, there is an opportunity to step aside (big yawn) from the daily grind, the daily pursuit, the daily frustration, those things that lead to disease processes within the body and in the mind. Step aside from all of that and sit in a chair, if we might, in the place of spirit and look and see ourselves on our path in the physical plane as a Soul, and innumerate, maybe on a piece of paper, those aspects of your Soulic life that you feel you can identify. Learning humility might be one. Realizing the evolution of the Soul might be another. Deep service to humanity might be another, and then get more specific if possible to see what actions would support that. What are those things you feel deeply that need attention, that have not had adequate attention?

For once one's list is complete, one needs to visit that list at least weekly. It sounds like a teacher in the schoolhouse doesn't it, Dear John? To visit the list weekly and to remind oneself what it is that transpired in the previous week that supports those goals or objectives or what it is that is coming up in the following week that would support those goals and objectives.

For by paying attention to the fact that we are eternal, that we can affect our own evolution, that we can affect the evolution of human kind, is a profound realization and from my place here, as a transitioned one, Dear John, there is no greater realization than that we are part of a lot longer event in life, if you call it that, in spirit. The wonderment of all this is that we ever believed. Few, no matter how studied they are, have connected to the notion of the long, long-body and see this as a schoolhouse, your time on the planet and actually reduce that then to assignments, if you wish, in the schoolhouse on a weekly basis of which I speak.

For it is that—quite simple—it is that simple, and yet for many it is that complex because many will find that their mind turns away from their daily pursuits of money, power, position, recognition, those things that stroke the ego.

The ego essentially gets parked during these discussions with oneself for it is those discussions that will allow the development of this list, and this list is very important for it sets in place, at least at one point in time, when it was written, those things that are in pursuit for you personally, of support of your long-body, the evolution of your Soul, and the evolution of humankind.

And as I see it now, Dear John, there is nothing more important, for it is the pinnacle, the height, the top of the mountain that we can look down into life, both from the physical plane and from my place in the world of spirit and see that we are part of something very much larger, not to be squandered at death of course! How childish that is in some respects. For death, as we are finding out, has only meaning for the physical body. It has no meaning for who we basically are deep within, within the Soul.

So, on this pinnacle, as we look around with our list of things and ways we can serve, we need then to commit ourselves to seeking to fulfill the items on the list at some level. To cause them to be in control of our entire life? Absolutely not! For there are many physical things to do in the earth plane that really have little to do with the perpetuation of the Soul's development and yet are required for physically being present on the earth, food comes to mind, exercise comes to mind, reading, writing, and arithmetic kind of things come to mind.

And yet this other layer is every bit as important and may be more important in the longer run for most, the layer of the Soul. Its intention for you, your recognition of that, your writing of activities that you might do to support that intention and that intention is found through the passion that you feel for those highly charged things in your life that seem to have nothing to do with earth plane in a sense, because when the passion takes over all the rest disappears.

Know of the artist who paints through the entire night, and you know several, John, almost in a trance.

Know the writer who, like yourself, gets caught up in the flow of the energy, the passion of the words that come through.

These are callings. These callings are passion. They are callings of the Soul.

And how might one respond in this list we speak of?

By writing down the opportunity of having time to allow those to open, to allow your body and your mind to quieten, to allow them to flow through so that they can respond. The musician who picks up an instrument and literally floats away into their own heaven through passion, through the Soul's request that the music, the vibration of the universe come through that person, and so it will.

So there is no end to this. Some speak at a gathering, and you have experienced this once yourself, Dear John, where your outer mind disappears and you become essentially a channel and that of course is one of your callings, and you have now found a passion for your duel body and so it is.

So there are many ways to listen to yourself, searching back to those times of heightened interest, of heightened energetic, of a true sense of love of life to find out the passion and know that the passion comes from the Soul and that the Soul's journey here through this classroom suggests that you do what passion speaks to as many times as you can, finding time for it, putting it on the list, assuring yourself and your Soul that you are attending to its long,

long evolution, that you are attending to the evolution of human kind by expressing who you are, uniquely who you are in response to the passion that has been brought forward through you. For it serves many. The service goes way beyond your Soul. There is no mistake here, Dear John, the services, the Divine services to many for each individual fits into this pattern, this long, long pattern. We are all connected, as you will recall, with these funny filaments of communication.

So, as we express our Soul's passion, we communicate that to all around us, both past and future, and it energizes it all. It is part of the mechanism of life and spirit and on the earth plane.

So, I ask as we bring this material to conclusion the time be spent in dedication to the work of the Soul, to the work of this long-body. For the transitioned ones support that. The bodies, of course, that go back through parents and parents and parents and will go forward through children and children and children and the Soul that comes in and out of these various bodies, the various Souls that do that each, seeking a platform for expression in the school-house, seeking to learn, to be elevated if you wish through these cycles to a new place, to the natural development of themselves in concert with the magnificent energies which we could call God or the High Spirit.

From where I am, Dear John, one might wonder how could I have missed all of this?

Why is it that it is not spoken of?

The mind is an amazing device for it captures our attention because we believe it is us.

We believe we are our mind.

We believe the mind runs the body.

We believe the mind is what allows us to work in life and defend it.

We believe the mind, somehow in an analytic process, guides our life.

What we have learned over these last several months is that from the world of spirit, that is completely incorrect.

The mind has analytic ability obviously, has verbal ability obviously, and can deduct and induce and these kinds of words obviously, but far deeper within us and behind the level of the mind is the Soul and its activity. It may be most active during sleep but it is always active, seeking to stimulate the body toward the objectives that it brought forward to be incarnated.

Were it not for the ego and the interference with the mind's strengths, through the ego, the Soul would speak as the sole voice of the body and its evolutionary process and things would be quite different, but then so would life in the schoolhouse.

So, it is not the schoolhouse to be changed.

It is not the mind to be changed.

It is merely stepping back, as I was unable to do, until I passed, except for sporadic times of course, but in any sincere way, any depth, I was unable to see what we are speaking of and feel it is so urgent for humankind today. Maybe as never before. But who am I to say that? For now is the time of great need for many, to step way back and look at this in a bigger perspective.

One of religious bent might say, Is this all God had in mind? This life of being born, working and raising children and dying through illnesses?

The answer, of course, is Absolutely Not.

Behind it all is the world of spirit and the magnificence of the Soul carrying energy and wisdom into the earth plane, the schoolhouse for the development of the Soul, for the development and evolution of the Soul as a contribution to the development of humankind. And in that perspective, for me, all makes sense, but I missed it until here.

Maybe being repetitious, if I could make this one gift to human kind it would be that they move back long enough, for those that are ready, to see this bigger picture for it is wondrous, wondrous, wondrous. The majesty of life as seen from the standpoint of the Soul's evolution in the schoolhouse, using the body as a mechanism for being in planet, is an amazing view of life, adds meaning to it all, great meaning, great love.

For what is there once one sees this longer body, this enormous loving contribution that we can make in the earth plane to our Soul's development.

Will the mind battle this on occasion? Absolutely!

Will the ego battle it on occasion because it cannot be proven in the earthly court of law? Absolutely!

And so it has been, and that was the creation of the cul-de-sac. When the magic of religion was unable to solve all the earthly problems many abandoned it and then many have tried to return and they are getting close and I wish them very well.

For this is not about a religious preference. To me this is about spirit and Soul and nothing else. And in there is the Divine impulse from God, that all of us are important, all of us are unique. We each are being asked in this manifestation on earth to bring forward to the schoolhouse who we are deeply and work with that, maybe on the weekly basis I suggest. To watch it, to develop it, to intend its betterment, to intend its betterment while we are here and to work past and through the cul-de-sac, not to be trapped in the cul-de-sac of "is this all there is?" but open the end of the cul-de-sac up as you get there, if you get there and when you get there and say...

"I'm not doing cul-de-sacs. I'm walking on through the cul-de-sac and opening the path for the children that follow, for the neighbors that hear and above all for spirit that wishes and wants nobody trapped in a cul-de-sac but rather opened to the entire flow of who they are into eternity, for it is the development of life unending. It is the development of life with infinite wisdom. It is the development of life incarnate and disincarnate, in balance, working

together to create the objective, if you wish, of the Divine
energetic that is supreme."

I speak then, Dear John, in closing of something that
would approach a prayer…
And that is from my place here in spirit…

I would pray that those who hold or
read this book, that may be attracted by
my celebrity, understand that the voice
within this is the voice from spirit and
that that carries an energy and the prayer
continues, that those who hold this book
and read this book be touched and each
in their own unique way by the opportunity of stepping back to perceive life as
eternal through the Soul, that there will
be many incarnations, that there have
been many incarnations, for each holding
this book is eternal from the Soul's
standpoint. And further as I pray that

each holding this book or reading this
book will adapt just a portion of their
earthly life to the realization that this is a
schoolhouse, this earthly experience, a
schoolhouse to learn to be affected by
life and to support the evolution of their
Soul and to know beyond all else that
how they live life affects their Soul, responds to their Soul's impulses, to the
evolution of their Soul, and to the evolution of the collective consciousness and
Soul of humankind. There is no greater
gift than that sight, the sight of the Soul,
our part in connection with the Soul. The
Soul's evolution being affected by our
actions in life on earth and knowing that
this time here on earth is yet a speck in
our own evolution and that we can put
the fear of death away as an abstraction
created by human minds in favor of the

understanding that the Soul is merely returning to its next assignment, the next
time in the place that I am, the wonderful
world of spirit.

So be it all, Dear John.

And thank you for bringing this forward. Thank you,
thank you, thank you.

JOHN—*Hume that was beautiful. This is John, as you
know.*

HUME—Dear John...thank you. As you can tell from
your reaction deeply heartfelt, using an earthly expression,
and what an honor it is for both of us to be called forward
to bring this information, this perception forward, for those
who may be in touch with this writing, called however
they are to it, whenever, for it is immortal, eternal and so
yes it is important that it be taken into the world and I
know you will.

Following some questions and answers about details I, John, ask: Is this all over? Are we done?

HUME—With the major transmissions? Yes.

With working together on bits and pieces, I am always available. And I suggest that when you return from your trip to the wonderful island that you love that we talk more about where you are and progress, realizing that much has been left in your lap on this earth plane. Know also as we discussed that it is part of your own Soul's destiny to be a channel and to bring material out into the world and so this service is service to your Soul.

For in servicing a higher calling, or of life, in life, a Divine impulse if you wish, to affect many, many lives, many more than you can imagine, Dear John, for we can see, because I hold the book. Many languages also...

But enough for now, so that the complications do not overwhelm.

In send you my deepest love and thanks.

Know I am with you, as are many, many others, with great energetic support.

For now, our blessings.

Susie sends two "blow kisses."

And I send them back—not them back—I received them; I send three back.

Ahhh…She smiles…

For now then…

VIII

Afterword

Hume-8 — 11/26/08, Newport Beach, California, 13:00

Good morning, Dear Hume, this is John, the day be-fore Thanksgiving, the 26th, a couple of minutes before our appointed hour of 9 o'clock.

Let me start by saying how absolutely blessed beyond belief I am to be partnering with you as essentially a chan-nel or intermediary in bringing this magnificent material through from spirit to what I call the earth plane.

And though it leaves me with the complications, such as they are, of carrying the material to the greater audi-ence, I feel that the energies behind the work are more than sufficient and our acumen is more than adequate to have that happen over a few months period. And then what pride we can all take as we see the energies of the books around the world doing their work, as they will, and I will be asking you please to report on what you see from where you are.

Ahhh, Dear John, this is Hume.

Your care and openheartedness is a wonder for me to watch, for as you approach this you approach it with your heart wide open and a sense of wishing the communication to affect many and, Dear John, it will.

You and I have been chosen to bring through information from the greatest spirit that is needed and is somewhat unparallel in the current communication with humankind from its source. And what a gift that is. And as a so-called celebrity I can't imagine a time more important in my existence to bring forward this material of the highest calling.

Each piece in this is mandatory in the sense that the energies must be passed from place to place. I have brought them through to you, you have brought them through to paper—well actually to recorders and to paper. As that paper is moved into book form, with a tiny bit of cleansing, and a lot of your love, it will continue to carry the energies of this greatest spirit, for you and I in integrity leave the energies alone, wish them well, and send them wonderfully on their way, like a sailboat in a wonderful breeze, to navigate as they will through their energies, to the energies of these books into people's hearts and Souls and stimulate, over time, new thinking, new possibilities and new openness and a willingness amongst many to stand up within themselves, to speak for themselves, who they are, what they are and as they see life from their Soul's perspective they will view it differently than it is currently being viewed and for almost any society in the world this will cause change. And the change will be to the purity of living with the energies of the Greater Spirit in a greater way.

Perfect? Never.

Substantially improved? Absolutely!!

And at the time now of great, great need, for there are these critical times in the history of the planet, particularly with the planet being as small as it is today, in communications, in warfare, in economics and on and on. The cultural clashes that could happen are enormous, for we are nowhere near a homogenized planet of love.

It is to you, Dear John, that I take off my hat.

And I return that, Dear Hume, with enormous respect.

Let us leave this then today as the end of what we might call chapter one of our relationship. As I mentioned it has been very smooth.

I, Hume, agree with that.

It has been wondrous for you, as a novel experience. For most sent you to the islands of Scotland or Hawaii and as you know I have sent you to the home on the Southern California coast. Strange, interesting, different and it reminds us of the wonders of all these forms of energy and how they work.

For you were tooled, dear one, to work in Scotland as you have many, many times now and to work in Hawaii as you have, both in Honaunau and in Kihei.

Now in Southern California. So know of your opening flexibility and that wonderful clean channel and that you and I now have completed chapter one in this sense of bringing through what needs to be brought through until you have time to have editing work done, that minor touching of the words and other information brought forward so that we can bless it before it goes to print.

Worry not about contacting me for I am always available to you. I know you do because you consider that a burden to me, but it is not a burden.

It is with great love that I receive your message to speak and I will always respond. Know that, Dear John, know it at all levels.

For I am part of your greater energetic family, work-mates if you wish, across that invisible line that we speak of that the Souls cross over at will and that the man wonders about.

Ahhh here we go again, but let's not. Let's leave it at that.

It will leave you feeling clean as you move through Thanksgiving and to Hawaii and you are clean, the work is clean, your understanding is clean. The steps ahead will be easier than you believe and they need be taken by somebody such as yourself of high integrity and you have that and a connection through me to it, which is the nature of this double channeling that is going on, in a sense not a great deal unlike the Druidic Iona experience, except maybe more vertical than horizontal—well, without that.

Let us say adieu today…lots of love.

Susie sends four kisses back.

And I return five to her.
Love you my love!!

And she says, listen carefully to what she said in your prayer room about fretting…love, love, and love.

Thank you, Hume. Thank you, Susan.

I'll be in touch, as I need to. It won't be immediately but you will know. You know what I am doing. And I am glad for this little time together for it acknowledges the closure maybe we needed…useful…full of love.

Blessings, blessings, blessings…

Susan ("Susie") Tettemer and Hume.